Days of Your Youth

A Fresh Look at Ecclesiastes for Today's Youth

GEORGE STATHEOS

Ark House Press
PO Box 1722, Port Orchard, WA 98366 USA
PO Box 1321, Mona Vale NSW 1660 Australia
PO Box 318 334, West Harbour, Auckland 0661 New Zealand
arkhousepress.com

© George Statheos 2021

Unless otherwise stated, all Scriptures are taken from the New Living Translation (Holy Bible. New Living Translation copyright© 1996, 2004, 2007, 2013 by Tyndale House Foundation. Used by permission of Tyndale House Publishers Inc., Carol Stream, Illinois 60188. All rights reserved.)

Some names and identifying details have been changed to protect the privacy of individuals.

Cataloguing in Publication Data:
Title: Days Of Your Youth
ISBN: 978-0-6451080-3-3 (pbk) 978-0-6451657-7-7 (ebk)
Subjects: Study; Ecclesiastes; Youth;
Other Authors/Contributors: Statheos, George

Design by initiateagency.com

For Dim

"Enjoy life with your wife, whom you love." Ecclesiastes 9:9

My Children: Karis and Silas of whom I am so proud

"*Let your heart give you joy in the days of your youth.*" Ecclesiastes 11:9

Arthur, Margie and Paul Statheos
Mum and Kathy.

ACKNOWLEDGEMENTS

ευχαριστώ για τη βοήθειά σας αντίο
Thankyou very much
Katoomba Christian Convention, for providing the opportunity to give talks on Ecclesiastes and to serve over the many years
Jonathan Dykes and Andy Stevenson from KCC
Mamre Anglican School Community
Cathie Graydon
Anne Bell
F1 team
Loren Shaw
Stephen and Shareen Liggins
LT and Belinda
Broadie
David Burton and Family
Ryan Willcockson
Wol Peeters
Kirk Patston
Iain Provan
Sam Chan
Ray Galea
Kerryn Baird
Zeus the dog for eating draft 3
Ark House Publishers

CONTENTS

Acknowledgements 7

Foreword 11

Introduction 13

Chapter 1 19
Life often seems meaningless and short

Chapter 2 27
We seek for answers in the wrong places

Chapter 3. 35
The Teacher describes the seasons of life

Chapter 4. 47
How we are made for eternity

Chapter 5. 55
Jesus' teaching on the wise and foolish builders as a strong foundation for life

Chapter 6. 61
How wealth can blind us

Chapter 7 69
Hope for youth in this hurting and confusing world

Chapter 8 85
Who can straighten out this twisted world?

Chapter 9 93
We will be young we will all grow old

Chapter 10 103
The consequences of forgetting your creator

Chapter 11 113
Jesus our rescuer from Judgement

Studies on Ecclesiastes 121

Endnotes 153

FOREWORD
KERRYN BAIRD

I had the privilege and honour as a young adult to be a youth leader with the amazing George Statheos, as part of a team which worked with over 200 high school kids. It was exciting and important work—young people emerge from childhood with lots of questions about the world and their place in the world. This is a time of life where there should be space to ask hard questions and seek real answers before the busyness of 'real life' takes over. Our youth group was a safe place to ask difficult questions and to learn that there was more to life than just our own perceptions.

Now that I am a mother, making time to ask the hard questions seems even more pressing. My teenage son said to me recently that he felt depression and anxiety are his generation's greatest problems. Today, the rise of social media means there are more opportunities for young people to connect with others than ever before, but research reveals that this form of 'connection' is also linked to loneliness, social anxiety and depression.

Young people need to be able to express all their concerns and fears with people who can show them there is a meaning and a plan for them when all about them seems meaningless and confusing. They need more than to be told to 'look inside' them; they need more than 'looking outside' by comparing their lives to a friend's shiny image on an Instagram post. They need to know that they matter in an ever-changing world that provides more questions than answers.

I was so excited when George told me he was writing this book. 'Meaningless! Meaningless! ... everything is meaningless' is the famous opening of Ecclesiastes, a book that often gets overlooked. George has the ability to take this ancient wisdom and make it accessible and relevant to today's world. Not just young people, but all of us have our moments when existence does seem bleak, but George takes us through this book showing us the true meaning of life: that we can rest on God's promises and that He will take our hands and show us the way.

Our young people need to know that there is safety and security in the knowledge that there is much more to this wonderful life God has given them.

INTRODUCTION

I was in the car the other day, supervising my daughter as she was learning to drive. On her playlist, the Adele song, *When We Were Young*, came on. I found myself feeling emotional and started to think about my school years. In the days that followed, I contacted some of my old school mates I hadn't seen for twenty years. We talked, we laughed, we reflected. Adele's song is all about being older and as she sings about being at a school reunion with all those people she had both loved and disliked, Adele reflects on how you bring your past into your present. I really connected with what she was singing about – when we were young. Much like the title of this book, "Days of Your Youth."

I remember first hearing about Jesus as a 17-year-old. Some 5 months later I became a Christian. Those teenage years had a profound impact on my life in so many ways. It wasn't until years later that I understood the significance of my becoming a Christian in the days of my youth.

Some 70% of all Christians come to faith in their teenage years[1]. This says an awful lot about the teen years being a period of your life where things are shaped and moulded, laying the foundations for the future.

I still remember reading the book of Ecclesiastes for the first time. I wondered why the book was even in the Bible. When you start digging a bit deeper, you see that it has a lot to say about purpose, life, judgement and choices.

Ecclesiastes is a profound book that speaks to these very issues. It explores the Big Questions of life:

- Where do I find purpose and meaning?
- Everything seems to be meaningless and fleeting; it's here and then it's gone. How am I to live in this ever-changing world?
- What is the purpose of humanity?
- How should youth make sense of this life?
- Is there life after this life?
- Where do I find the answers?

As Ecclesiastes does, we will refer to the author as the Teacher. He explores every pleasure you could imagine and concludes that everything is meaningless. He describes life in all its seasons and how much of it seems to repeat itself – life has its cycles. Many books in the Bible are about the life to come, but Ecclesiastes is about the here and now. The gospel message of the New Testament brings to life the book of Ecclesiastes.

Consider what the book of James has to say: "Why, you do not even know what will happen tomorrow. What is your life? You are a mist that appears for a little while and then vanishes." James describes life as short, 200 years after Ecclesiastes was written.

In the book, the Teacher describes the twistedness of sin and how having a firm foundation in life gives us hope. The Teacher is searching for answers to the meaning of life. In the final chapter, Chapter 12, he comes to this profound conclusion: he reminds us to "remember your creator in the days of your youth". This is his summary as he reflects on himself, reflects on his life and the things he has pursued. Remembering God is what ought to shape our lives.

The Teacher calls to us with a sense of urgency of the shortness of life, and why it is so important to remember God *now*. It is not like remembering if I have forgotten my sports gear or the name of the girl I am on a date with; this is a much more significant remembering, a call to be mindful.

Why does he say that it is in our youth that we need to remember? Because this is where your life is shaped. These are formative years. The reason we need to remember is because we forget. Even secular culture acknowledges this with truisms like: "if you fail to remember the past, you are doomed to repeat it".

Your teenage years are short. They are a mere breath. Believe in God before the days of trouble, especially before you enter adulthood, with all its distractions and demands. These distractions only get bigger. Your heart gets harder, and you become stuck in your ways. That is why it is critical that we need to lay the foundations of our faith now, rather than later.

The writer goes into detail about growing old and what it looks like: it is the opposite of being young. This is a period of life where crucial decisions are made that shape the rest of your life. Questions like: Who will I marry? What job will I pursue? How will I spend my money? Should I stop going to church? Is there hope for youth in this ever-changing world?

If you keep putting off the decision to follow Jesus now, you may never stop deferring it. You say, "I'll do it tomorrow," but tomorrow never comes.

Let our creator God shape your life now. You don't know when the day – the day when you will have to face your creator – will come.

The things I learnt in the days of my youth have helped me immensely in my adult life. They have helped me deal with hardship, rejection and disappointment. This is the conclusion of the matter, says the Teacher: "Fear God and keep his commandments, for this is the whole duty of people" (Eccl 12:13). The decisions we make now will have consequences when we face that final day and stand before our Creator and His judgement.

These reflections on Ecclesiastes will examine life and its purpose. They will encourage youth to see the importance of making decisions now, while you are young. I've written this book for young people who know that Jesus is the meaning of life and that living for Him is our purpose, and for those seeking meaning; for youth leaders, those in their twenties, for parents with teenagers, and for schools as they teach Christian studies. This book is an opportunity to consider the meaninglessness of the here and now and how this meaninglessness makes it all the more important for young people to find true meaning in Jesus.

In the back of this book you will find a study guide to help you think through what the book of Ecclesiastes has to teach us.

You will find it helpful if you read Ecclesiastes before you read *Days of Your Youth*.

Currently, George is working as a Chaplain at Mamre Anglican School; he has previously worked as a youth minister and as a lecturer in Youth Ministry. He is married with two teenage children.

My Dad and me my son and me
Generations come Generations go

CHAPTER 1

Life often seems meaningless and short

*"Meaningless! Meaningless!"
says the Teacher.
"Utterly meaningless!
Everything is meaningless." (**Ecclesiastes 1:1**)*

*For the message of the cross is foolishness to those who are perishing, but to us who are being saved it is the power of God. (**1 Corinthians 1:18**)*

In writing a book for youth, I had fun remembering what it was like to be a teenager. When I was a 15-year-old in Year 9 of high school, my best friend was Robert. We did everything together. We would often stay at each other's houses for the weekend.

One Saturday morning, we woke up and came up with this hare-brained scheme to embarrass people. We got a wallet and a $5 note with the money hanging out of the wallet a bit. We tied some fishing line to it and put it on the footpath outside my house. Robert and I hid inside my parents' bedroom. From there we could watch the whole event unfold. The road we lived on was a major thoroughfare.

Our first victim was a man walking along the footpath. He saw the wallet, looked around to see if anyone was watching, then bent down slowly and put out his hand to pick it up. As he reached out his hand, we pulled the fishing line towards us. He reached out again and we yanked it a second time. Then the man stood up scratching his head, and the wallet went down the driveway like a rabbit going down a hole. The wallet went up the wall and into the window, with us opening the window and Robert and I yelling out "Scab!" What a joy!

The second victim was a lady pushing a pram. We let her pick the wallet up and then yanked it out of her hand with the fishing line. The third victim was a jogger who went past the wallet at first. Then he came back, bent over to stretch his hamstring, and reached out – just as we yanked it back down the driveway. This

> Is there anything of which one can say, "Look! This is something new"?

is what my life looked like as a 15-year-old, full of immaturity. But how these years go by ever so quickly.

MEET THE TEACHER

The Teacher of Ecclesiastes is not writing about his life as a young person. Instead, he is reflecting back, wanting us to learn from his observations on his years of youth.

The book of Ecclesiastes is about a Teacher reflecting on the journey of King Solomon's life. Ecclesiastes simply means a place of gathering where someone is teaching about God, much like a church (*ekklesia* in Greek).[2]

> **The eye never has enough of seeing, nor the ear its fill of hearing.**

At some point in their life people will ask, *why am I here?*

"Meaningless, everything is meaningless, says the Teacher (*Qohelet* in Hebrew)".[3]

Wow, what a way to start a book! Is this going to be a depressing book or a more reflective one? The book of Ecclesiastes gives answers, but does not dodge the tough issues. The word in Hebrew for meaningless is *hevel*.[4] The writer of Ecclesiastes is not saying that life is without meaning, but that life is fleeting.

From God's perspective, our whole lifespan is merely a breath; here one minute, then gone. Life is a gift from God; we don't control how many days we have to live. The word *hevel* comes from the life of a man in the Bible called Abel who had his life cut short. His life was taken from him way too early by his brother, Cain. That's why his life is meaningless, because it was a mere breath.[5] His life was fleeting, similar to a young person dying in a car accident. They were taken away too early; we say they had their whole life ahead of them. This word meaningless (*hevel*) is so important and it appears 33 times in the book.⁶

PEOPLE COME AND GO

A friend of mine asked me to spend a few hours on the weekend helping him concrete his driveway. As a Greek, I should have been happy about concreting, but the day was hot and long, and what was meant to be a couple of hours of fun took the whole weekend. "What do people gain from their labours" (Eccl 1:3)? We work hard and we don't know what we gain.

My father worked hard and saved his money to enjoy retirement. He planned what he wanted to do, where he would go and who he would see. He died, mowing the lawn, never able to do those things he had looked forward to. What did he gain?

"Generations come and generations go" (Eccl 1:4). I recently farewelled my senior students, some of whom I taught from the start of their school life until the end. Then a year later another generation has come and gone. I have done this approximately 25 times. It seems as though that time has gone far too quickly. Life is short. I find myself mourning the loss of the years I taught those students. It seems to me that those years should not have gone so fast.

> I have seen all the things that are done under the sun

The Teacher says you will never know everything. You will come back from that overseas trip and realise there is always more to see. You study and there is always more to know.

"What has been will happen again." (Eccl:9,10). Look at anything 'new' – it has really happened before. Some things come and go ever so quickly. What happened to planking? How long will Tik Tok and Snapchat be around for? What will come after Gen Z? Nothing is new. Look at fashion: My wife, Dim, and I went to an engagement party and those in their early twenties were dressed in the 80's look. Apparently, it's back – I thought it never left! I was 'in' because I still wear clothes from the 80s that I never got rid of. Take jeans, for example; we have in style straight fit jeans, skinny, boot cut, flare, boyfriend, baggy, ripped. We now have the 'new black' in fashion. I didn't know that black could be darker than black!

> but I learned that this, too, is a chasing after the wind.

The Teacher describes how life moves in cycles, saying there is "nothing new under the sun". This theme keeps reappearing throughout the book. There is nothing new; we've done it and seen it all before. We forget previous generations and what they have achieved.

Do you know who Edwin Flack was? He was the only competitor for the Australian Olympic team in the 1896 Olympics and he won 2 gold medals. Robin Williams, in that legendary film *Dead Poets Society*, takes his students to the honour board list of those who have come and gone. He tells them to "seize the day": this is *hevel*, a breath.

LIFE SEEMS MEANINGLESS

What am I doing here? Life is as fleeting as mist, it can be easily missed. It is as though you rush all day, only to miss your train. Life is like washing the dishes. You do them, then you have to do them again. You finish an essay and another arrives. Life goes around and around with no gain.

The Teacher says life is like "chasing after the wind" (Eccl 1:14). You can't catch life and keep hold of it. It's like a treadmill: you're forever running, but never getting anywhere. Someone achieves something, yet it has already been achieved.

> **I said to myself, Come now, I will test you with pleasure to find out what is good.**

In 1953, Edmund Hillary and Tenzing Norgay were the first to reach the summit of Mount Everest. At the time, people said would no-one would ever do it again, but in 2019 alone, 807 people made it to the summit.

Australian swimmer Chloe McCardel has broken the men's world record for the most swims across the English Channel. She has swum it 35 times. Again, people said that the time of 2 hours would never be broken for the marathon. I watched it get broken in 2019.

Some of you may ask the question, where is God? He is not distant. God is present under the sun. The apostle Paul says that God reveals Himself so that we "…would seek him and perhaps reach out for him." (Acts 17: 27). Many people try to find meaning "under the sun" (Eccl 1:14). But if life is short, what do we live for?

There is nothing new under the sun.

CHAPTER 2
We seek for answers in the wrong places

*"I denied myself nothing my eyes desired;
I refused my heart no pleasure."*
(Ecclesiastes 2:10)

"Therefore, as God's chosen people, holy and dearly loved, clothe yourselves with compassion, kindness, humility, gentleness and patience."
(Colossians 3:12)

*E*cclesiastes is about the futility of our attempts to get the most out of life. The Teacher tries everything but it all seems to backfire. His efforts show that you want more, but you are never satisfied. The ancient Greek philosopher, Plato, said we are all "leaking vessels that will never be filled".⁷

RE-RUNS

"I know," the Teacher says, "the answer is in pleasure and getting the most out of life. I'll become a hedonist" (2:1). In every facet of life, I'll pursue feeding my ego. Let's try laughter and entertainment! I'll go to the Apollo Comedy Festival. What about watching re-runs of *Big Bang Theory* or episodes of *Brooklyn Nine-Nine*? We may watch the re-runs of these shows, but even they start to become a bit monotonous when you can say the punchlines before the characters do.

> I wanted to see what was good for people to do under the heavens during the few days of their lives.

How about some all-night benders, mixing drinks on my own or with friends? Maybe drugs are the answer to my boredom? I have the money to try all these things. These pursuits start to consume the lives of many young people who can never say no. There are too many followers in life. I have the money, so I will pursue material possessions, accomplishments, projects, achievements. I won't do a PhD, I'll buy one at the University, better still I'll buy the University, says the Teacher.

You could buy a bigger house, or do renovations. My wife and I arrived at a wedding function early, so we decided to go for a walk around Darling Point. We came across a house that had just sold for 52 million dollars!

I HAVE IT ALL, AND MORE

The Teacher thought, I will invite loads of people on Facebook and invite them to my parties. I will Tweet, Facetime, Zoom, Snapchat and Instagram.

As a family, we wanted a breed of dog that few people had, so we researched and chatted to dog lovers. Finally, we bought a Cavoodle. I had never seen one of those before. I took him on his first walk and everyone seems to have one.

> I undertook great projects: I built houses for myself and planted vineyards.

The teacher says, I will amass silver and gold. I will be wealthier than everyone else. He tried money "but never has enough" (Eccl 5:10).

He saw the best orchestras and bands play at the best concert halls. My wife and I were once invited to watch Handel's Messiah at the Sydney Opera House. Her friend was performing in a lead role and gave us free tickets. I was so excited, as all this was new to me. My only other concert experience at the Opera House was seeing a Russian Violinist. No one told me about the clapping etiquette; I clapped in all the wrong places. I cheered like you do at a footy game. The stares I got!

We showed our tickets to the usher and my wife was escorted to the private box while I was directed to the back row. What an amazing experience, hearing the music, even from the back row. "He shall reign forever". The message behind the music was so powerful. It sent shivers down my spine.

How are we to process these things in life? God gives them to us for enjoyment and pleasure. We swim in God's beaches, we ski in His snow, we enjoy His sun. But are we grateful? We need to appreciate God's good gifts to us.

The Teacher commends the enjoyment of life, "because there is nothing better for a person under the sun than to eat and drink and be glad. Then joy will accompany them in their toil all the days of the life God has given them under the sun" (Eccl 8:15").

The Teacher says, I will try and find meaning in sexual pleasure, in pornography (if it existed then). A 17-year-old boy who is a Christian was told by a work colleague he wished he had waited to have sex. He said he had so much sex with different girls that it meant nothing to him anymore.

> **I denied myself nothing my eyes desired; I refused my heart no pleasure.**

I have everything and everyone knows it. I will drive my Lamborghini or Porsche in a ritzy area and watch heads turn as I stop at traffic lights, even when they are green.

I gave myself everything, I did not deny my heart anything. I looked at all these things I had done and tried: it's all meaningless.

Like lots of these material things, they promise a lot but leave you spiritually empty. You end up trying something else that only lasts a season (Hebrews 11:25). So, you pick up something else that seems to fall through your fingers without satisfying you.

When I first left school, I had a job operating a printing press. Every Thursday when we got paid, a bloke I worked with would use all his pay to buy something. One week it was a surf ski that he only used once, next week it was gym equipment, then a mountain bike … the list went on. I own some of these things as well. The point is he spent thousands of dollars using things once and thinking those things would bring him meaning, but they never did.

GIFTS FROM GOD

How can we get the most out of life, then? The Teacher tried everything and found it left him empty.

> Then I turned my thoughts to consider wisdom,

We get the first glimpse of this reccurring theme at the end of Ecclesiastes 2. Enjoyment comes from God, so does knowledge and happiness (Eccl 2:25-26). These are all gifts from the hand of God: your friends, bike, car, phone, job. Our salvation, which cannot be bought or earned, is a gift from God. It's hard to imagine – we don't deserve this free gift of God! Yet he gives it to us abundantly (Ephesians 2:8,9).

When I was at Bible college, I used to go to a state high school to teach scripture with my colleagues, Ross and Dan. One day, I asked a year 9 class this question: "If you died tonight and God asked you why He should let you into heaven, what would you say to him?" The students wrote down their answers:

- because I've been christened
- because I'm a good bloke and I once prayed
- I go past a church on my bike, when I go to the shop
- I gave money to a charity
- because my sister goes to a private school (that's the first time I've ever had that answer).

> I saw that wisdom is better than folly, just as light is better than darkness.

Most of the answers started with 'I', but I explained to the class that the correct answer to the question is "because Jesus died for me". I explained that it's not what *we* do, but what Jesus has done by his death, that enables us to get to heaven. The bell went and everybody had left except one boy. I was surprised because he was normally the first to leave, but this time he was the last. He pulled out a piece of paper and got a pen and asked me to say the answer again. I said to him "Because Jesus died for me".

He wrote down what I said, put the answer inside his wallet and started to walk out. I asked him what he was doing and he replied, "Don't you get it sir? I have my wallet with me all the time. If I get hit by a bus this afternoon, I'll have the answer on me."—as if he could use it like a travel card. He didn't understand that salvation is God's free gift, but he gets 10/10 for creativity. We cannot contribute to our salvation. Be a thankful gift-receiver. Appreciate what God gives us (Eccl 5:19). You can live for Jesus and never worry about assurance of salvation. That means we don't have to **do** something to get to heaven because it has been **done**.

Ecclesiastes is all about embracing God and all He gives. Are you someone who recognises all that God gives? Some times we look at God's gifts and we forget how great they are.

I took some Fijian friends to see the Three Sisters in the Blue Mountains. They screamed with excitement. They said, "It is all fantastic! What a view!" I was like, "yeah, it's not bad; been here before." When we truly recognise all that God offers, we want to live for him.

In the book of Acts, we see Saul as a young man. He thought he had the truth, but Jesus appeared to him in person and he instantly realised that Jesus is the Truth. As an old man, Paul makes three *I am* statements (Romans 1:14-16).

"(**I am committed** both to Greeks and non-Greeks, both to the wise and the foolish. That is why **I am so eager** to preach the gospel also to you who are in Rome.

For **I am not ashamed** of the gospel, because it is the power of God that brings salvation to everyone who believes: first to the Jew, then to the Gentile.")

Paul came to realise that everyone can hear this great news about Jesus. It is not only a message that saves, but is a message that transforms from within. Paul could testify himself by how Jesus changed him from hatred to love. The Teacher would have been overwhelmed of how clear the message could be. This happened to me when I was taken to a youth group where I heard I could have eternal life. I gave my life to Jesus when I was 18. My older brother had done it 3 months before me. Ecclesiastes is about the Teacher searching for the truth and meaning. Paul is all about the truth ultimately finding him on the Damascus Road and there is no need to search for the truth anymore. Prior to Paul's conversion he thought it was all about his impressive CV: where he was born, the religious duties he performed. But when he became a Christian he dumped in the rubbish on bin night all those things he thought were important, to be taken to the tip where they belong. All he wants to know now is the power of the resurrection. (Philippians 3:4-10)

Season for every activity, a time for

CHAPTER 3

The Teacher describes the seasons of life

"There is a time for everything, and a season for every activity under the heavens:"
(Ecclesiastes 3:1-8)

Be very careful, then, how you live—not as unwise but as wise, making the most of every opportunity, because the days are evil.
(Ephesians 5:15-16)

I once saw an Xbox ad on YouTube. A mother is in labour and the child is born and goes flying out the window, through the air. The child then becomes a teenager and gets older the further he travels. Finally, as an old man, he lands in a grave. Then the slogan comes through – "Life's short, play more: Xbox."

It is a clever ad. Even Xbox recognises that life is short. But they don't have the answer. Statistics tell us on average we live 79 years, we spend 27 years sleeping, 7 years trying to fall asleep, 100 days laughing, 4 and half years eating, 8 years watching tv, 11 years screen time, 13 years 2 months at work, 1 year 30 days romance, 4 months brushing our teeth, the list goes on.[8] Then there are 8 years left over.

HOW ARE WE TO LIVE IN THIS SHORT LIFE?

There is a time for everything, and every season is different. The Teacher says that the world operates and is understood by seasons. Even in the first chapter of the Bible the seasons and their role in creation are described (Genesis 1:14). Seasons have a function and a pattern. The Teacher knows there is a time for harvesting; you sow and reap crops. He describes human experiences in this chapter in positives and negatives. They are polar opposites. Life moves in these cycles.

"A time to be born and a time to die" (Eccl 3:2). Life can be like two bookends where you have a beginning and an end. "A time to plant and a time to uproot." You may move to a new suburb, a new house, a new school, a new job. You might have a realisation that things are not all that well, that you have been sowing the wrong seeds in your life. Planting the seeds of the spirit will bring a positive change as you see the fruit of love, joy, peace, forbearance, kindness,

> God gives wisdom, knowledge and happiness

A Time for Everything

goodness, faithfulness, gentleness and self-control grow in your life (Gal 5:22-23).

One of the saddest things I have to do in my line of work is to conduct a funeral. It's even worse if the funeral is for a teenager. Youth today are confronted way too much with unnecessary death. Within weeks of the birth of my son, my father passed away.

The Teacher says that we will all die, no one will avoid it. But while we wait to die we should live full lives. In John's gospel these words are taken to the next level, where Jesus says, "I have come that you may have life, and have it to the full" (John 10:10). God gives life, full life to those who believe. There is no uncertainty. God's word says that if you believe in Jesus, you will have life to the full.

Are you living the way God wants you to live? Are you excited about the things of God or about the things of the world? Ultimately you learn that worldly things are not fulfilling and they lead only to emptiness.

There is a time and a season for every activity under the heavens: a time to kill and a time to heal, restoration in people's lives, forgiveness. I was told by a friend recently that there had been a falling out with a sibling that went on for 15 years, over a will. They reconciled recently.

A student told me that she had really negative people in her life. I still remember what she said to me: "Sir, I had to cut them out of my life". It was consuming her life. She took assertive action that worked.

This one we all identify with: "a time to weep and a time to laugh", sometimes we don't know which one to do. Is this a season of mourning for you? Maybe you find yourself grieving the loss of a loved one or a friend and you do not know how to move forward. Remember, Jesus wept when his friend Lazarus, died even though he would be brought back to life.

CHANGING SEASONS

Jackie is grieving for her teenage years which were taken from her due to abuse. She has shared that in recent times joy and laughter have returned to her life. She said to me,

> *"Do you rise above your past*
> *and make a difference,*
> *or do you remain controlled*
> *by your past*
> *and make excuses?"*[9]

a time to be born and a time to die

A friend said to her that over a period of months, she could see she was leaving one season and entering another. The Teacher talks about a season of celebration. We don't know why things happen the way they do, but the Teacher says that life happens in seasons.

"A time to scatter stones, a time to gather them" (Eccl 3:5). The early church had a time of growth and a time of scattering to other parts of the world. The nation of Israel went through a similar thing with the exile. Some people are only in our lives for a season and they move on. There is a time to embrace or hug and a time to refrain.

"A time to search and give up" (Eccl 3:6). Sometimes you have to just let people go. Some people spend their lives searching, looking for the perfect relationship. My wife knows a lady who thinks a man is going to fill her emptiness. Every six months she's in a different relationship and thinks that he's "the one". Jesus meets a woman just like that by a well in John 4. She has one husband after another. Jesus says to her they cannot fulfil in a way that will satisfy her. She was a woman who was shamed because of her past. Jesus says nothing about her past. Only the true living water can satisfy. Apart from Jesus, everything else is futile.

> **a time to mourn and a time to dance**

Maybe you need to confront someone but first take the log out of your eye. Perhaps you need to listen or encourage someone. Sometimes you know the right thing to say but don't have the right words. "A time to speak and time to be silent" (Eccl 3:7).

"A Time to love and a time to hate" (Eccl 3:8). Do you hate sin? I love that passage where Paul says the 'greatest of these is love' (1Cor 13:13). Which one controls your life more: love or hate?

Last year four children: Antony, Angelina, Sienna, from the same family, and Veronique, a cousin, were killed by a drunk driver as they walked along the footpath. If any people ever had a right to be angry or have hatred in their hearts, it is the Abdallah family. They have faced so much grief and loss. Weeks after the tragedy happened, the parents said the most remarkable thing; they said that they did not hate the man, but forgave him. The parents had the assurance that their children were in a better place…paradise.

Let love reign.

A SEASON OF WAR

Sometimes you can only have peace after war. Then the Teacher says about war, "wisdom is better than weapons of war." There are options other than war. We only need to look at the impact that war has had on individuals and countries. It is to be avoided at all cost. My father fought in the Korean War. He returned home but the effects of the war never left him.

Here is an example of a war worth fighting for: my wife does some volunteer work helping to equip people to make a stand against the sexploitation of girls and women. Sadly, many teenagers have been saturated with sexualised thinking for such a long time that they don't even recognise the effects it has on their attitudes and behaviours. The leaders of this army of volunteers are constantly battling against those who promote this misogynistic ideology. Their call for action seeks to inform and motivate young men and women to fight this battle with them.

Life does not follow a script that we can predict. But we do know that God is sovereign; He rules and He is in control. As this proverb says:

> *"The king's heart is in the*
> *hands of the Lord. He guides*
> *it like a river wherever*
> *he pleases"(Proverbs 21:1).*

a time to tear and a time to mend

No one can discover God's plans from beginning to end.[10]

I have taken about 6 service trips to Fiji. Gen Zs love them, the students are very hands-on. In our Western culture we love destinations and are not concerned about the journey so much. We just want to get ourselves there because we are impatient. We had a long trip ahead of us. I asked my Fijian friend Sisa how long the trip would take. His response was, "When we see the sea." So, I asked for him to explain it to me in hours and he replied, "Five hours." He also told me, "George, the trip is part of the journey. Enjoy it!"

"God has made everything beautiful in its time" (Eccl 3:11). We see God's glory in this life, and in the next we will see it in his fullness.

SEEING GOD IN ALL SEASONS

This does not mean that every season is joyous. Our problem is that we're not always happy with the season we are in. We sometimes have a problem with seeing God in each season, especially if it is a season we don't enjoy. But the apostle James tells us that God is at work even in the difficult seasons of our life. He says:

> *"Consider it pure joy, my brothers and sisters, whenever you face trials of many kinds, because you know that the testing of your faith produces perseverance"* (James 1:2-3).

Different seasons in life are opportunities for spiritual growth. If we learn and grow through each season, we can then offer wisdom from our experience to others going through the same season. What comfort it can be to someone if we share our wisdom, insight and compassion with them. It is all about sharing with others what we have learned, and what the Lord has taught us, through our different seasons of life.

Four years ago, I was diagnosed with Parkinson's Disease. It hit the family pretty hard. What will my world look like? How do we process this? What will this season look like? Trust in God's goodness, even though that is hard to do, at times.

We contemplate: why do I have to go through this season? Life is unpredictable, messy and frustrating. We need to look to God and trust Him even when His purpose for taking us through a particular season is not always clear.

> **I know that everything God does will endure forever**

SEASONS OF GROWTH

A dear friend of mine threw in his faith because he did not like the season he was in. This is a great tragedy, not only because he turned his back on God's offer of salvation, but because he also made his suffering harder, by no longer trusting that the Lord was using this season for his good.

I love those mining shows where they drill, sift through soil, and dig for gold. Others dig for gems, precious stones. They bring in heavy machinery and drill for years on end, often with little reward. Sometimes they hit it big and share their spoils with the workers.

One story told of a man who panned the streams and found fragments of gold. He believed there was gold to be found in the surrounding hills and mountains. He hired workers, bought specialised machinery and mined for ten years, barely making enough money to get by. In the end, he sold everything off. The man who bought the mine from him struck gold five weeks later! In hard times, persevere: there may be blessings just around the corner.

> God will bring into judgement both the righteous and the wicked

A SEASON FOR YOUTH

I read these verses to a twenty year the other day.

"Though you have made me see troubles, many and bitter, you will restore my life again; from the depths of the earth you will again bring me up.[21] You will increase my honour and comfort me once more"(Psalm 71:20-21).

This is a great Psalm which alludes to a season of healing where God will bring restoration in the hard times. We may have felt pain, loss, confusion, disappointment, rejection, depression and anxiety, but God wants to bring healing to those dark times.

> **So I saw that there is nothing better for a person than to enjoy their work**

What season of life are you in? Do you look for opportunities for God in every season? I have a friend Helen, who lost a child. It was a hard time for her and her family. In the midst of all the pain they never lost sight of Jesus. Theirs was a season of great sadness.

Not every season appears in Ecclesiastes 3. As humans, we often look back to previous seasons with regret or happiness and we want to revisit the past seasons, instead of looking to the present. Sometimes in life, all we talk about is the past; we can't look beyond that. We can get locked into thinking about a certain period of our lives. It sometimes seems like we only talk about past seasons at church, remembering camps and events, instead of talking about the present or praying about the future.

Young people, don't let your past control you or let people control you. I know a 17-year-old girl who was badly bullied. The harassment followed her from one school to another. After lots of prayer and counselling she had the realisation that it was simply about the bullies' insecurities and had nothing to do with her.

One difficult season of life can prepare us for the next season. Sometimes the seasons of life are intertwined, sometimes they're not. Sometimes we go through life stages that are completely different from one another. But of this we can be sure: this too shall pass. Everything has a beginning and an end. Even a difficult season will pass. The important thing is that we learn to trust that the Lord has something to teach us in every season.

> **I saw the tears of the oppressed— and they have no comforter**

The world changes rapidly. Our world is currently in a difficult season of a pandemic. Are you still looking to God and sharing His love? People need to hear about Jesus, no matter what is happening on our planet. What will the next season bring in your life? We do not know, but God does. Trust him.

God has set eternity in our hearts

CHAPTER 4

How we are made for eternity

He has made everything beautiful in its time. He has also set eternity in the human heart; yet no one can fathom what God has done from beginning to end.
(Ecclesiastes 3:11)

Whoever believes in the Son has eternal life, but whoever rejects the Son will not see life, for God's wrath remains on them.
(John 3:36)

I know you won't remember New Year's Eve 2000, but I certainly do, since it was the day before I got married. For everyone else, the most memorable part of the New Year's celebration was the Harbour Bridge lit up with the word *Eternity*.

It was there as a tribute to a man, Arthur Stace, who features in the story of Sydney's history. Arthur Stace heard two sermons, in 1930 and 1932, that challenged him to think about where he will spend eternity. He decided he wanted to spend eternity in heaven with Jesus and wanted everyone in Sydney to share his hope. Arthur Stace was illiterate. He couldn't read or write. But he picked up a piece of chalk and taught himself to write the word 'Eternity' in beautiful copperplate script. Then he walked around Sydney for 35 years and wrote 'Eternity' over 500,000 times—on the footpaths and brick walls—to remind people that there was more to reality than the short life we live here and now.

The Teacher in Ecclesiastes says that God has set eternity in the hearts of people. God has made us for eternity. There is much more than this life. If life is short, live for what matters.

> Two are better than one, because they have a good return for their labor: If either of them falls down, one can help the other up.

Every couple of years I have to upgrade my First Aid qualifications. During a coffee break, I found myself talking to our instructor about how he got into being a first aid trainer. When I asked the question, he started to unbutton his shirt right in front of me. I felt awkward, as did the other people around me. When he'd finished unbuttoning his shirt, I saw there was a scar all the way down the centre of his chest. He told me that 9 years ago, when he was driving home on a wet day, he lost control of his car and crashed into a wooden fence. A paling pierced his chest and he should have died that day. But the first person on the scene of the accident had done a first aid course. They kept him alive until the ambulance arrived. He decided that he would live his life to pursue what saved him.

WHAT DO YOU LIVE FOR?

The Teacher gives us a glimpse of what is to come, beyond this short life: eternity. But many choose to spend their life chasing earthly desires, as if this short life is all there is, with no regard for eternity.

Maybe we misunderstand what heaven will be like. The parable of the hidden treasure tells us how great heaven is going to be. Jesus tells a story (parable) of a man who goes out to a field. He finds a treasure in the field and is so excited about the treasure (Matthew 13:44), that he sells everything he has so he can buy the field. Do you recognise how important this treasure is? Jesus is talking about eternity. When people find out about him and what he offers, they sell everything to spend eternity with Him. Have you realised the great treasure we have in Jesus? It's like the disciples Peter, James and John, who start to recognise who Jesus is and what he gives when they have an incredible catch of fish (Luke 5:1-11).

> **Better a poor but wise youth than an old but foolish king**

We get frustrated in life by not having the big picture ourselves. We want to look into our own crystal balls to see what's ahead so we can have more control. Life isn't like the Netflix series *Troy*, where there's a pantheon of gods on every street corner, and even mere mortals can influence and manipulate them.[11] "Our message to the world is to abandon striving after control and to embrace the one who is in control".[12]

The God of the universe has the big picture and we have to trust Him. Whatever the season you are in, acknowledge God. Only God controls the times and the seasons, and only God's word contains wisdom that speaks to every season we may go through.

Two thousand years ago, God gave us this big picture in understanding eternity. Does it matter how we live out these seasons of life? (Eccl 3:17). The Teacher says that it does matter, because there will be a Judgement.

Paul says to those in Athens (my relatives) who believe in Greek mythology, "For he has set a day when he will judge the world with justice by the man he has appointed. He has given proof of this to everyone by raising him from the dead" (Acts 17:31). Jesus' defeat of death demands that we live for Him. Nowhere in Greek mythology do we hear about someone conquering death. Some believe while others mock Paul's message. We must keep in mind that this is the first time they had heard about Christianity.

> **Guard your steps when you go to the house of God**

Being a Christian means we trust in Jesus, not just for a season but through all seasons, in every stage of life. As Paul says to Timothy, "preach the word in and out of season" (2 Tim 4:2). For Christians, every season is relevant. There is this urgency with what we say to others. The good news of Jesus needs to be preached not just when we feel like it, but in all seasons.

ETERNITY AWAITS

Eternal simply means forever. Hell will last forever, heaven will last forever. Whether we spend eternity in heaven or hell comes down to our choice. I once had a student say to me, "I can't wait to go to hell because all of my mates will be there." I said, "Sorry to disappoint you. In hell they won't be your friends, friendship is a gift of God." Heaven will be such a great place. I know lots of people that hurt in this life. Heaven will not be a patched-up earth. I once owned a white Nissan Pulsar. Coming up for registration, I noticed rust appearing at the bottom of the doors. I bought some "bog" that panel beaters use. I sprayed white paint over the top and no one noticed it was a patched-up job. Heaven won't be a patch-up job, it will be all new.

> **Do not be quick with your mouth, do not be hasty in your heart**

> "He will wipe every tear from their eyes. There will be no more death or mourning or crying or pain, for the old order of things has passed away" (Revelation 21:3-4).

The verse we started with at the beginning of this chapter is John 3:36. Where we spend eternity has to do with how we respond to God's Son. The Teacher in Ecclesiastes would have been blown away by the teaching of Jesus.

To understand what it means that Jesus died for our sins, think of it like we are wearing our own black shirt, which represents sin and death. Then Jesus comes along and offers us His white shirt, which represents forgiveness and eternal life. If you reject the white shirt, you keep the black one, which leads to death. If you accept the white shirt, it leads to eternal life.

Whoever believes in the Son has eternal life, but whoever rejects the Son will not see life, for God's wrath remains on them.

WHAT WE BELIEVE NOW AFFECTS ETERNITY

Hebrews 9:27 tells us that we're "destined to die once, then face Judgement". God will call each of us to give an account of how we have lived our life under the sun. Notice it is not a second chance or third: "to die once".

When we die we will stand before God. What would your life's pursuit be if you knew you were about to die?

We must live our lives under the sun for God. Life never works with us acting as creator, for we are not in control. Have you ever attempted to do something that was beyond your ability? I once asked my brother who was going to the dentist to get some fillings done, if he wanted me to do it for half price. I told him I owned a drill. For some reason he said no. What a disaster that would be if I were to fix his teeth! I have no qualifications, no training, no equipment, no idea and now, a brother with no teeth.

We cannot reconcile ourselves with God. It is beyond anything we can do. Only Jesus can.

Wise person who built the house on rock

CHAPTER 5

Jesus' teaching on the wise and foolish builders as a strong foundation for life

> "I saw that wisdom is better than folly, just as light is better than darkness."
> *(Ecclesiastes 2:13)*

> "Therefore everyone who hears these words of mine and puts them into practice is like a wise man who built his house on the rock".
> *(Matthew 7:24)*

The wise life, the Teacher says, bows to God in the highs and the lows. It is about making the right choices in life that have consequences for yourself and others. As Job says, why only thank God in the good times. "What about the bad times." We become very good at thanking God for the things that come from his hand. Not hard things of course, God would never do that to us.

When times are good, be happy; but when times are bad, consider this: God has made the one as well as the other. (Eccl 7:14.)

In October 1997, I took a busload of teenagers to Thredbo on a school excursion. As I was getting off the bus, the students all suddenly went silent. I looked around and saw why everyone was quiet. Several months earlier there had been a landslide on the Alpine Way. Eighteen people died, and a man named Stuart Diver was the only survivor. Every student knew what they were looking at. His wife sadly died in the landslide. (Interestingly, his own brother, Ewan, was part of the rescue party searching for survivors).

> **As goods increase, so do those who consume them**

Years later, the coroner gave his verdict of why this tragedy occurred: heavy rain and leaking water throughout the years beneath the resort had compromised the foundation. The foundation is everything, and if it falls, everything built upon it will crumble.

Jesus finishes his first public talk called the Sermon on the Mount in Matthew 7. He tells a story about two builders building their houses. One builder was wise, and the other was foolish. The two houses looked the same at first glance, just like newly-built suburbs all look the same. The difference between these two houses was that one had a foundation of sand, but the other was built on rock.

Just as a solid foundation is important to support a house, we need to build our lives on a firm foundation. When the storms of life come—the hard times—they will expose our foundations. A weak foundation may not show up as cracks in your house for years. My sister's house ended up with some huge cracks in it, caused by heavy storms. I bought some Polyfilla to fill the cracks. The whole tube disappeared into the crack without filling it! It needed a cement mixer.

BUILD WELL

If you build your life on the wrong thing, it will fall with a great crash. Society says to build your life on things that it claims will last, but never do (like my first car – it got nicked before I even drove it). In Ecclesiastes 2:13, the Teacher talks about trying this approach, and its failure to satisfy or bring meaning to our lives.

The wise life stops and listens to God's word, and puts Jesus' words into practice. Wise men and women build their houses on rock. Jesus is saying that his life and words are the rock, the firm foundation to build your life on.

Christians still face storms. Some friends of mine have gone through shocking times. Having that firm foundation in Jesus gives you strength in those difficult times under the sun. As the Teacher says, "wisdom is a shelter" (Eccl 7:12). It is above us, a firm protection. Don't be like the foolish man or woman, who hears these words but does nothing about them (Matt 7:24). Your foundation may not seem important now, but it will later. Jesus provides the best foundation. Life

> **Everyone comes naked from their mother's womb, and as everyone comes, so they depart.**

is short, it is *hevel*. "Seek first his kingdom and his righteousness" (Matt 6:33).

Jesus is concerned not only that we build our life on Him as our firm foundation, but that we also count the cost of following Him so we will be faithful to the end. He says,

"Suppose one of you wants to build a tower. Won't you first sit down and estimate the cost to see if you have enough money to complete it? [29] For if you lay the foundation and are not able to finish it, everyone who sees it will ridicule you, [30] saying, "This person began to build and wasn't able to finish" (Luke 14:28-30).

We have all seen houses that are half finished in our neighbourhood. There is one I see on my walks, that remains half finished. The purpose of this parable is to help us understand that we can't skimp on our commitment; we can't be a part-time follower of Jesus; we can't pick and choose what matters and what doesn't—when we will follow Him and when we'll just do our own thing. If we don't give our all to Jesus, we will end up with a half-built house that is no good to anyone. Following Jesus is a lifelong commitment.

FOLLOWING JESUS

In Luke 5:1-11, we read about a group of fishermen who have been out fishing all night and haven't caught a single fish. Jesus tells them to put their nets out in deep water. They obey Jesus and the most incredible thing happens: they catch so many fish that their boats begin to sink and their nets begin to break. Most importantly, "all his companions were astonished at the catch of fish they had taken, [10] and so were James and John, the sons of Zebedee, Simon's partners.

Then Jesus said to Simon, "Don't be afraid; from now on you will fish for people." [11] So they pulled their boats up on shore, left everything and followed him. Those early fishermen were so amazed by Jesus that they left their nets behind and started to live their lives following Him.

You may be someone who has just started following Jesus; keep growing in your love for Him. If you are not sure about following Jesus, keep reading about Him. The New Testament book of Luke is a good place to start. Remember, we have the Holy Spirit who helps equip us on our journey.

Whoever loves money never has enough

CHAPTER 6
How wealth can blind us

"Whoever loves money never has enough; whoever loves wealth is never satisfied with their income."
(Ecclesiastes 5:10)

"What does it profit a man if he gains the whole world and loses his soul?"
(Matthew 16:26)

In 2004, I watched an episode of 60 Minutes. It was about a man called Larry who won 185 million dollars in a lottery: the largest lottery win ever. Several years later, the 60 Minutes crew wanted to see how winning that amount of money had changed his life. What fascinated me most was his answer to the question, "If you could have your old life back without the 185 million, would you?" Without even thinking, he said "Yes!" He told the interviewer about the impact that the money had had on his life: he lost friends, and people only wanted him because of his money.

> A good name is better than fine perfume

PEOPLE PURSUE WEALTH

The danger of wealth is that it is deceptive. When I saw that episode, I said to myself that it would be different if I had won the money. That is the deceptiveness of wealth.

Listen to what the Teacher says: "Again I looked and saw all the oppression that was taking place under the sun: I saw the tears of the oppressed and they have no comforter; power was on the side of their oppressors and they have no comforter" (Ecclesiastes 4:1).

In his sermon on the mount, Jesus' first words are, "blessed are the poor in spirit". In the ministry of Jesus there was always this contrast between the rich and the poor. In the book of Mark, we are told about a rich young man who comes to Jesus. Note he is young and wealthy, which was very uncommon. He asks what he must do to inherit eternal life. Jesus says to do what the commandments say. The man responds that he has kept them all since he was a young man. That is a pretty tall order, to have kept them all. Jesus replies that he should sell his possessions and follow Him, and the man goes away disappointed.

The man was wealthy and his money was his idol. His wealth was consuming him. On one level, he was looking for the right answers in the right place: if you want a haircut you go to a hairdresser, not a butcher's shop. But there is a commandment that the young man had failed to see: "You must have no other god's before me" (Exodus 20:3). We are told that he went away sad because he loved his money.

Whoever loves money never has enough money. Jesus could have said, *Sure, come to me on your own terms. That'll be fine! We could probably do with some financial support for my public ministry.* But Jesus was not interested in the man's money – he was interested in his soul. The man wanted eternal life and Jesus could give it, but the man's money was his god.

A god can be anything; it could be a relationship, it could be a sport or a job or any material possession. We're supposed to use things and love God, but we are tempted to use God and love things. As the American pastor, Timothy Keller, says, "the human heart is an idol factory".[13]

Jesus made the point to the rich young ruler that nothing can ever take priority over Him in our hearts and lives. He says, "where your treasure is, there your heart will be also" (Matt 6:21). Jesus wants us to treasure him above our material possessions, above our family, our money, and our dreams. Whatever we prioritise in life, that is what we love the most. Jesus wants us to love Him the most and put Him above all else.

> It is better to heed the rebuke of a wise person than to listen to the song of fools.

When my son was about 11, he went to his team's end-of-year soccer BBQ. They had a trampoline and everyone wanted a turn. The father said only 3 at a time. They put up with this instruction for a while, but in the end more and more players hopped on the trampoline at the same time, until the whole team was on it. You could see the whole thing buckling under the strain until it finally broke under their weight. I noticed something was wrong when a spring rocketed past my head.

Young people, the world tells you that any number of things can be your god—money, sex, power, fame, sporting prowess, career, social media and success. But these idols cannot bear the weight: they're false gods. They can't love, forgive, give us hope, or save us. You can name them what you like, but they will buckle and break because they are not solid foundations on which to build your life. Nor will they lead you to eternal life with Jesus—quite the opposite.

> The end of a matter is better than its beginning, and patience is better than pride.

"Whoever loves wealth is never satisfied with their income" (Ecclesiastes 5:10). I knew a billionaire who confessed to me that he was never satisfied with what he had. He remembers as a young man making his first million, but he wanted more. He even told me he was greedy.

The Teacher talks about the danger of those who have too much wealth. It blinds them and prevents them from seeing the poor and those who have too little. The Teacher says "give the poor justice" (Ecclesiastes 5:8). And the book of Proverbs says, "Whoever oppresses the poor shows contempt for their Maker, but whoever is kind to the needy honours God" (Proverbs 14:31).

CONTENTMENT

They are powerful words. I have friends who seem to have so little in comparison to me but are happy with what they have.

We must learn to be thankful for what God gives us, whether it is a little or a lot (Philippians 4:12). In this short life we have been given, let's seek to help the poor and make a difference. As the early Christians said in Galatians 2:10, "Continue to remember the poor, the very thing I had been eager to do all along."

The key life lesson about money is contentment. I have a Fijian friend who gets paid four thousand dollars a year. He has 3 daughters, aged 18, 20, and 24; 2 cousins and his wife, who all live in a 2-bedroom house. He is content with what he has.

> **Wisdom, like an inheritance, is a good thing and benefits those who see the sun.**

We played soccer against a Fijian village after school. It was "Australia v Fiji"; what great afternoon fun. We decided to give away two soccer balls to the best boy and girl. They came forward and we made a presentation. Then something very strange happened. Both children went to the back and gave the balls to an elderly man. I asked my friend if that was their grandfather. He said he was the chief of the village and this act meant we all share the ball, no one owns it. As I reflected on what they did, I thought if that was me who won the ball, I would have kept it. What a lesson in sharing. Youth, constantly recognise what we have belongs to God. Share it with those who are in need.

How true it is that naked a person comes from his mother's womb, and naked they depart. You can't take anything with you (Eccl 5:15). George Swanson died at 71 years of age. He wanted to be buried in his Corvette car. The car could not fit in a grave plot, so they made the plot bigger for the car to fit. He was buried at the cemetery in his yellow Corvette with his seat belt on. I don't think he will be burning round in heaven in his Corvette.

God is the one that gives a person his wealth (Eccl 5:19). Consider the parable of the rich fool in the book of Luke. The man builds bigger and bigger barns for all of his crops, then sits down and says, "Look at what I have achieved." This man's life is the epitome of someone chasing after the wind. He is a fool because he thinks his wealth is his own doing. The parable explains that God gave him his fertile soil, and yet he never thanked God for it. He is remembered not as a wise man, but as a fool, because he hoards the Lord's blessings for himself and is not rich toward God. Or consider this parable from Eccl 9:15-16:

> "There was once a small city with only a few people in it. And a powerful king came against it, surrounded it and built huge siege works against it. ¹⁵ Now there lived in that city a man poor but wise, and he saved the city by his wisdom. But nobody remembered that poor man. ¹⁶ So I said, "Wisdom is better than strength." But the poor man's wisdom is despised, and his words are no longer heeded."

> **When times are good, be happy; but when times are bad, consider this: God has made the one as well as the other**

I watched an episode of Bondi Rescue where a group of young people were caught in a rip. The lifeguards managed to save all of them. You would think the first people who would go and thank the lifeguards would be those that were saved. However, the sad reality is they walked away without saying thank you.

The picture we get from the story we are told in Ecclesiastes, is about an old man who saved everyone who lived in the city. Once again, no one remembered the man or thanked him. We must not treat God the same way. We should show gratitude and be generous toward God and others, in response to the generosity He has shown to us.

Young people, as you make money in years to come, be generous with it: give to the Lord's work and support Christian charities that seek to help the poor.

Lecrae, Hope for youth

CHAPTER 7

Hope for youth in this hurting and confusing world

4:13 Better a poor but wise youth than an old but foolish king who no longer knows how to heed a warning.
(Ecclesiastes 4:13)

Don't let anyone look down on you because you are young, but set an example for the believers in speech, in conduct, in love, in faith and in purity.
(1 Timothy 4:12)

The Teacher says to "guard your steps" (Eccl 5:1-2). In other words, watch where you put your feet, don't just follow the crowd in life. Jesus talks of a wide road and a narrow road. Most people go down the wide road. They're totally oblivious to being on the path to destruction, but they like being on the road nonetheless. Maybe they think, "We must be right: there are so many people on this road." They are so busy on the wide road they don't even notice the narrow road. But, Jesus says the narrow road leads to life – watch out for the exit sign!

> Whoever fears God will avoid all extremes

Most afternoons I drive up the Great Western Highway, which is a three-lane highway. Then there is a narrow road to the left, which is called the Explorers Road. You don't really notice it until you need it. "Path after path will be relentlessly explored ... In the end, only one way will be left."[14] There are some who see the narrow road but choose the wide road.

SEEKING WISDOM

One of the challenging issues about being young and genuinely seeking the truth is that you may be susceptible to different trends and philosophical thinking. In the search for meaning and being open to learning about different beliefs, we can sometimes listen to the wrong voices.

Heed the Teacher's advice to "search out wisdom" (Eccl 7:25). The book of James 1:6 tells us if you lack wisdom ask God and he will give it generously. Look at the Scriptures, as Timothy was encouraged to. In Proverbs 1:17 we are told that understanding begins with God and that is wisdom. "The fear of the Lord is the beginning of wisdom." Wisdom is not intelligence or strength, but putting God in His rightful place.

There's a man in John 3 who's looking for truth. His name is Nicodemus and he's a religious leader. He knows a lot about religion, but knows nothing about a relationship with God. He misunderstands wisdom for head knowledge. He comes to Jesus in the cover of darkness so no one will see him. Jesus tells Nicodemus that no one can see God's kingdom of heaven unless they are born again.

Jesus says that if someone wants to go to heaven, they must be born again. Not 'maybe': the process of being born again must happen in people's lives. This passage leads on to the most famous verse in the Bible, John 3:16: "For God so loved the world that he gave his one and only Son, that whoever believes in him shall not perish but have eternal life." In Ecclesiastes, the Teacher wants to assure us that we must pursue wisdom all the days of our lives. That famous verse reveals what the heart of wisdom is: the fact that God loves us and His love saves us from Judgement.

> **Wisdom makes one wise person more powerful than ten rulers in a city**

SOCIAL MEDIA: THE MODERN-DAY TONGUE

The Teacher tells us to watch our direction – are we on the right road? He says to watch what we say: "Do not let your mouth lead you into sin" (Eccl 5:6). "Do not be quick with your mouth" (Eccl 5:2).

Some pointers about the tongue:

- Think before you speak
- Treat others the way you want to be treated
- Use the right language
- Don't have regret

In an unhelpful situation:

Turn away
Walk away
Stay away

- Watch the tone you use
- Rehearse what you will say
- Send a written message or text
- Get advice from someone older
- Pray and ask God for help

The Teacher reminds us that our tongue, if we don't control it, can lead us into sin. Cain killed his brother because he never exercised self-control. The next point the Teacher makes is all about having a quick mouth, or sarcasm gone wrong. The problem with the quick mouth is that we can easily use words to bring people down. The Teacher says, "Words from the mouth of the wise are gracious, but fools are consumed by their own lips"(Eccl 10:12).

Many years ago, I spent a winter in Vancouver. I stayed with friends and they invited me to a young adult's church New Year's Eve party. We played Pictionary, and my partner was a guy called Karl. I was staying at Karl and his wife's house. Part-way through the game, Karl was drawing something and I could not make head nor tail of it. It looked like a spaceship. At the end of the round they explained to everyone it was a letterbox. Being Greek and loud, I said, "You call that a letterbox? That looks

> Do not pay attention to every word people say, or you may hear your servant cursing you

nothing like a letterbox. That looks more like a dinosaur being taken for a walk!" Then I jokingly yelled out, "Get me a new partner—I'm trading this one in!" Everyone was mortified. They could not believe that I would want a new partner. I had to explain the Aussie sense of humour has sarcasm, which was very different to the Canadian sense of humour. It really goes to show that what comes out of our mouth can sometimes be misinterpreted. It's good to be clear when explaining things.

BUILD OTHERS UP WITH YOUR WORDS

> I am determined to be wise—but this was beyond me

This story will highlight the power of words. Murray Rose was the Ian Thorpe of the 1950s and 60s in the pool, six-time Olympic medallist world record holder. He recalls a childhood incident that changed his life. As a young boy he was playing with his newly purchased boat in shallow water by a river. Without realising it the boat drifted away out of Murray's reach. He recalls his distress; an old man seeing his despair rowed over to get his boat, and returned it to him. The old man said to Murray, "Can't you swim yet?" "No", he replied. The old man looked at him and said "You will be a good swimmer." Rose recalls that those words sowed a seed in his life so that he wanted to swim.

The power of words.

The book of James also talks about words: the tongue, and bringing the tongue under control. James describes how small things can often control large things: a bridle in a horse's mouth controls the whole animal, and the rudder on a ship can turn the whole ship around. In other words, tame the tongue and don't let it control you: *you* control *it*. James gives more examples about the tongue:

> **So I turned my mind to understand, to investigate and to search out wisdom**

"With the tongue we praise our Lord and Father, and with it we curse human beings, who have been made in God's likeness. Out of the same mouth come praise and cursing. My brothers and sisters, this should not be. Can both fresh water and salt water flow from the same spring? My brothers and sisters, can a fig tree bear olives, or a grapevine bear figs? Neither can a salt spring produce fresh water" (James 3:9-12).

Let me put this in a modern context. I was driving on the M4 Freeway in peak-hour traffic in my car and noticed smoke coming out from the car in front of me. It started to impede my vision and that of the other drivers around me. I tooted my horn and waved to the driver in front, to warn him of the danger. Then I heard rattling noises coming from under my bonnet. It was my car that was the problem! I looked at the temperature gauge and the car was boiling hot. I managed to pull over in the emergency lane. I open the bonnet and steam poured out everywhere; there was so much steam I lost weight. I called the NRMA (they fix broken down cars) and it took the mechanic 30 seconds to find out what the problem was. The fanbelt is a small piece of rubber in a car. If it breaks (which they do) it can stop a car in its tracks and even seize an engine. It cost $10 to buy a fan belt. While it is broken, the car will overheat and not move at all. Unless of course—like mine—it gets towed away. Remember, something so small can cripple a car.

The tongue has been used since the beginning of time to manipulate words, to build up or tear down. Social media is the modern-day 'tongue': we say things, we post comments, and in the process, people are crushed and devastated. Some young people's lives are shattered by what others say to them online. Sometimes negativity is contagious; others start to join in with their harsh comments. We can hide behind a screen and say whatever we want, not realising the terrible impact our words can have.

I recently heard of another tragedy in which a teenager took their own life. It highlights how youth are searching for answers, but do not seem to be finding any. What a horrible situation young people find themselves in, when suicide seems to be the only option. The one thing that seems to be lacking in youth culture is hope, and the lack of hope affects resilience. No one seems to have the answers for young people. Hope is not part of their vocab.

the wise heart will know the proper time and procedure

Yet, the Bible tells us there is hope for teenagers. The word 'hope' appears 180 times in the Bible. It does not mean 'hope' as in "I hope you enjoy the movie". It means the anticipation of a future certainty. The Bible says we have incredible hope in the one who has defeated death.

"For you, O Lord, are my hope, my trust, O Lord, from my youth" (Psalm 71:5). I love this verse. It cements for us the idea that the assurance of hope can be shaped while you are young. There are very few certainties in life, but one certainty we can be assured of is God's forgiveness and the hope of eternal life for those who believe.

There is a movie about the surfer Bethany Hamilton, called *Soul Surfer*. On the day she lost her arm through a shark attack, she was supported by her friends who were with her when the accident took place. They used a tourniquet to slow down the bleeding. By the time the ambulance arrived, she was close to death. A member of her community was driving the ambulance that day. Despite being in shock, Bethany remembers what he said to her as he helped her into the ambulance: "He will never leave you." What is so incredible is that she remembered the Bible being quoted. What a promise from the Scriptures, that whether we live or die, God will not forsake us (Hebrews 13:5).

HOPE FOR YOUTH

"We have this hope as an anchor for the soul, firm and secure" (Hebrews 6:19). No matter what the world throws at us, we are secure because of the anchor.

> Anyone who is among the living has hope

"He has delivered us from such a deadly peril, and he will deliver us again. On him we have set our hope that he will continue to deliver us" (2 Corinthians 1:10).

Hope means you will never be abandoned. God is for you. He walks with us and gives us certain hope when we put our trust in Him. In this verse, the words *delivered us* appears three times. I think we can be assured He saves.

HEARING LECRAE

Sometimes in life you get to meet great people. I once had the privilege of meeting Christian rapper Lecrae, who has close to 2 million followers on Instagram. He performed a rap and gave a cracker of a talk at the school where I was Chaplain. He asked the audience whether anybody had money on them, and somebody held up a $20 note. He asked everyone how much it was worth. Everyone yelled out "$20"! He screwed up the $20 note, threw it on the ground and trod on it. Lecrae picked it up and asked how much it was worth now. They said "$20". We don't have to think too hard about what he meant. No matter what people say or do against you, it should not change who you are and how much you are worth in God's sight. Be sure that you hang around people who are going to treat you and value you for who you are.

In Psalm 139, King David describes how God knows us intimately: in our highs and our lows of life, when we are in a good or in a bad place. Read the Psalm and highlight the verses you like:

> "¹ You have searched me, LORD, and you know me.
>
> ² You know when I sit and when I rise; you perceive my thoughts from afar.
>
> ³ You discern my going out and my lying down; you are familiar with all my ways.
>
> ⁴ Before a word is on my tongue you, LORD, know it completely.
>
> ⁵ You hem me in behind and before, and you lay your hand upon me.
>
> ⁶ Such knowledge is too wonderful for me, too lofty for me to attain.
>
> ⁷ Where can I go from your Spirit? Where can I flee from your presence?
>
> ⁸ If I go up to the heavens, you are there; if I make my bed in the depths, you are there.

> **Wisdom is better than strength**

⁹ If I rise on the wings of the dawn, if I settle on the far side of the sea,

¹⁰ even there your hand will guide me, your right hand will hold me fast.

¹¹ If I say, "Surely the darkness will hide me and the light become night around me,"

¹² even the darkness will not be dark to you; the night will shine like the day, for darkness is as light to you.

¹³ For you created my inmost being; you knit me together in my mother's womb.

¹⁴ I praise you because I am fearfully and wonderfully made; your works are wonderful, I know that full well.

¹⁵ My frame was not hidden from you when I was made in the secret place, when I was woven together in the depths of the earth.

¹⁶ Your eyes saw my unformed body; all the days ordained for me were written in your book before one of them came to be.

¹⁷ How precious to me are your thoughts, God! How vast is the sum of them!

¹⁸ Were I to count them, they would outnumber the grains of sand—when I awake, I am still with you.

¹⁹ If only you, God, would slay the wicked! Away from me, you who are bloodthirsty!

²⁰ They speak of you with evil intent; your adversaries misuse your name.

²¹ Do I not hate those who hate you, LORD, and abhor those who are in rebellion against you?

²² I have nothing but hatred for them; I count them my enemies.

²³ Search me, God, and know my heart; test me and know my anxious thoughts.

²⁴ See if there is any offensive way in me, and lead me in the way everlasting."

> **The quiet words of the wise are more to be heeded than the shouts of a ruler of fools**

CONNECTEDNESS WITH YOUR CREATOR

One of the key things in helping teenagers with mental health issues is what we read in Ecclesiastes 4:10-12:

> If either of them falls down,
> one can help the other up.
> But pity anyone who falls
> and has no one to help them up.

> **Words from the mouth of the wise are gracious, but fools are consumed by their own lips**

¹¹ Also, if two lie down together, they will keep warm.

But how can one keep warm alone?

¹² Though one may be overpowered, two can defend themselves. A cord of three strands is not quickly broken.

Relationships are vital in life. Having the support of others in the midst of hard times gives you great comfort and strength. The Teacher highlights that having the support of someone else means that you are not alone. Isolation is one of the worst things you can face if you are suffering from mental health issues. One of the major things that helps youth is someone walking alongside them in those hard times. Not trying to give advice, but just being there. Sometimes just a supportive presence can be enough to help others. It is this connectedness we all need. The Bible describes us as being separated from God. Jesus is the only one and way that is able to connect us with God. You may find this hard to believe. When someone becomes a Christian, they become friends of the living God. We are able to call him Father.

There's a dude called Job in the Old Testament, who goes through a really hard time in his life. He has a group of friends who gather round him without saying a word for days. Their presence would have brought great comfort to him. But things go pear-shaped when they start to give him advice. They should have just sat there with him and not said a word. Saying nothing is sometimes the best advice: "Go near to listen" (Eccl 5:1).

A cord of three strands is not quickly broken.

FOR THOSE WHO WORRY

Jesus holding all those strands together in your life? Stress and worry often lead to anxiety. Listen to these profound words said by Jesus 2000 years ago:

"Therefore, I tell you, do not worry about your life, what you will eat or drink; or about your body, what you will wear. Is not life more than food, and the body more than clothes? Look at the birds of the air; they do not sow or reap or store away in barns, and yet your heavenly Father feeds them. Are you not much more valuable than they? Can any one of you by worrying add a single hour to your life? Therefore, do not worry about tomorrow, for tomorrow will worry about itself. Each day has enough trouble of its own"(Matthew 6:25-34).

Matthew 6 tells us, "Don't worry." He is not telling us to avoid any type of work that may lead to worry. But rather, to not let these things consume you or control your life.

One of the things that people worry about most, is their future. But the Teacher in Ecclesiastes tells us that no one can discover anything about their future (7:14). It's a good thing that God does not let us know our future…it's hard enough dealing with the present.

Too many of us carry the burdens of others. There is a difference between support and carrying the weight of others (Galatians 6:1-5). Young people, when you get overwhelmed with things, learn to say No. A friend of mine has this written on a plaque on his desk, to remind himself not to lose sight of what is important:

> **"Remember that the most important thing is that the most important thing remains the most important thing".**

Furthermore, listen to these comforting words that Jesus says to us:

"Come to me, all you who are weary and burdened, and I will give you rest. Take my yoke upon you and learn from me, for I am gentle and humble in heart, and you will find rest for your souls. [30] For my yoke is easy and my burden is light" (Matt 10:28-30).

The religious leaders at the time of Jesus would often make people obey laws that had no relevance to God. They would cause people to feel bad about themselves. It would make the religious leaders think they were more righteous than others. Have you ever watched a weight-lifting competition where it becomes obvious that someone cannot lift a particular weight? The religious leaders loved seeing people fail. Jesus is saying that His life is not a burdensome one. What He offers us is grace, mercy and peace, and there is plenty to go around.

> So then, banish anxiety from your heart and cast off the troubles of your body, for youth and vigor are meaningless.

At the start of this chapter, I quoted from the book of 1 Timothy, where Paul writes to a young Timothy: "Don't let your age affect what you can do for God." Be a role model, whether older or younger. Put on those leadership characteristics of love, faith and purity. Young people, look to your creator in tough times.

What is twisted cannot be straightened

CHAPTER 8

Who can straighten out this twisted world?

How do we make sense of this life?
"What is twisted cannot be straightened".
(Ecclesiastes 7:13)

Godly sorrow brings repentance that leads to salvation and leaves no regret, but worldly sorrow brings death.
(2 Corinthians 7:10)

I was once watching TV when I heard a banging sound from the other side of the house. I went upstairs to investigate the noise and found my son doing a jigsaw puzzle. I asked him about the noise, and he said that he was stomping a jigsaw piece so that it would fit. I told him it was the wrong piece, to find the right piece and it will fit.

God has made us for a purpose, and we function best living His way. Ecclesiastes 7:29 tells us: "God created mankind upright, but they have gone in search of many schemes". In Eden, humanity was perfect - there was no sin or barrier between us and God; they were free to live in the garden and enjoy God forever.

Then Adam and Eve wanted to be like God. Once they defied God and ate from the tree of the knowledge of good and evil, sin contaminated everything.

Once again, the book of Ecclesiastes paints only part of the picture. God will send in His rescue plan, Jesus; our perfect saviour, who was without sin. "But God demonstrates his own love for us in this: While we were still sinners, Christ died for us" (Romans 5:8). What a great demonstration of God's love. Young people, understand that in life when people don't love you, God does, and He went to a great extent to show you.

A TWISTED LIFE

There are so many young people who are broken, who are struggling with mental health issues. The Teacher says this issue is his issue as well: "What is twisted cannot be straightened" (Eccl 1:15, 7:13). When things are messy, we say to ourselves, "I can fix that." There are some things we can fix on our own or with the help of others. But we cannot straighten out our sin. Politicians are always trying to fix what is twisted: thinking that education is the answer, or that technology will fix us. But who can straighten or untwist this mess?

I once visited a man on his deathbed in hospital. He refused to believe he was going to die. He said to me, "Wait and see, I will be out tomorrow and we'll catch up then". He died that night.

> dust returns to the ground it came from, and the spirit returns to God who gave it

The Teacher would have longed for the day when the Messiah would straighten out the twisted consequences of sin, once and for all.[15] It is futile to think we can fix things ourselves. A student once said to me, "I know about Jesus, and I want to become a Christian. But let me straighten out my life first." I said to him, "You'll never straighten out your life." Only Jesus can straighten out our lives.

Things in all of our lives need fixing, and sometimes we don't even recognise when they do. A friend of mine has a faulty aorta. He lived for decades without knowing he had a problem with his heart valve, until he had a heart attack. Although he survived, he has a health problem that cannot be straightened out.

A LONG JOURNEY

On my very first service trip to Fiji, I got an infected finger. I don't know how it happened, but it throbbed for days, and it was so painful I was even kept awake at night. I was due to go to an island the next day with my Fijian friend, Sisa, and twenty others, on a small crowded boat. I was told it wasn't far. I learned afterwards that Fijians have a different way of measuring time, in which minutes mean hours. I have a confession to make: at this point in my life, I was 28 years old and I was a non-swimmer. I was filled with terror. The thought of going on a little boat to a small, remote island made me feel like the disciples on the boat with Jesus when He calmed the wind and the waves. Sisa said, "George, you are quiet. I have never seen you quiet. Are you all right? You are pale. Are you sick?" The trip took three hours and when we finally got onto the island, it was extremely good to be on dry land.

We attended a church service, did some leadership training and had a feast for lunch. But I didn't count on the trip back!

Because we'd overstayed, we left late at night, just as a storm came in. It started to rain and thunder rumbled ominously overhead, while lightning flashed in the distance. The waves started breaking over the boat. I thought the trip there was bad, but the trip back was far worse. I said to myself, "If I die, my mum will kill me." To complicate things, the captain of the boat was a ten-year-old boy, who was wearing sunglasses…at night!

> **The Teacher searched to find just the right words, and what he wrote was upright and true**

With no lights on the boat, I could not see a thing. Then the Fijian women—wait for it—decided to sing Hymns, yes Hymns. I thought this was neither the time nor the place.

Nearly five hours later, we hit dry land and I sat on the shore for what seemed like ages. What a great feeling that was.

I remember lying on my bed that night when something started to happen that I'd totally forgotten about: my finger started to throb again. It's not that my finger was cured for the day, it was more the fact that something more serious was at stake. My throbbing finger was insignificant in comparison to the boat trip. I still had a need to heal my finger, but I didn't even think about the throbbing when I thought I was going to drown at sea.

YOUR GREATEST NEED?

In the book of Mark, we read about a paralysed man who wanted Jesus to heal him. He heard Jesus was in town, at a place called Capernaum, so his four loyal friends carried him on a mat to see Jesus. But when they got there, the house was crowded with wall-to wall people, like Westfield on Christmas Eve. There was no disabled parking in Jesus' day. They couldn't get him inside because of the crowd, but they didn't give up easily. They carried the man onto the roof, made a hole (this may be the first recorded installation of a skylight in ancient history), and lowered him down. This would have been a great tweet.

The crowd was waiting for Jesus to perform a miracle and heal the man. But the first words Jesus said were, "Son, your sins are forgiven". These are strange words. If I was the paralysed man, I'd feel ripped off. The man just wanted to walk. He didn't realise that he had another, greater need. If we saw each other with God's eyes we would see that our greatest need in life is to have our sins forgiven.

> **Of making many books there is no end, and much study wearies the body**

Did the paralysed man have some hidden sin in his life we don't know about? I don't think so. The man simply wanted to walk again, but Jesus knew that the man's greater need was to be forgiven. So Jesus told the man his sins were forgiven, then commanded him to take up his mat and walk home.

The religious leaders were upset because Jesus said that He can forgive sins, but only God has the authority to do that. In saying "your sins are forgiven", Jesus implies that He is God. He demonstrates His authority by healing the man and telling him to pick up his mat and walk. By forgiving the man first, Jesus shows us that our greatest need in life is to be forgiven. If the man had died unforgiven, the consequences would have been eternal. To heal the man cost Jesus a word. To forgive cost Jesus His blood, cost Him His life.

The big issue is not whether the paralysed man could stand, but how he stood before God. He stood a pardoned man, a forgiven man.

No matter who you are or what you have done, Jesus can straighten it out. He can forgive you. Notice that when Jesus heals, He does so completely: the man does not limp out, but walks out strongly, even carrying the mat. When Jesus forgives, He does so completely as well.

> **Fear God and keep his commandments, for this is the duty of all mankind**

Relay, passing it on

CHAPTER 9

We will be young we will all grow old

'Remember your creator in the days of your youth'.
(Ecclesiastes 12:1)

"Continue in what you have learned"
(2 Timothy 3:14-15)

What a great reminder this passage is of thanking God for those who have had an impact on your Christian life. "But as for you, continue in what you have learned and have become convinced of, because you know those from whom you learned it, and how from infancy you have known the Holy Scriptures" (2 Tim 3:14).

The apostle Paul faithfully passed on the gospel message to Timothy and others. The relay baton was passed onto Timothy when he was young. Paul encouraged him to not be timid, to be bold for the kingdom despite his young age.

PASSING THE BATON

Listen to the words of another leader motivating youth to not hold back in sharing their faith: "Expect great things from God; do great things for God."[16] William Carey inspired a generation of young people to take the gospel to other nations, just as Paul did in his generation with Timothy. Look at some of the leaders in the Scriptures, that God has transformed to be incredible leaders. Sometimes I have found myself passing the gospel baton to someone who seems like an unlikely convert. Then I remind myself: that was once me.

In 1993, I was asked by one of my youth group kids if I would be interested in coaching four 16-year-old boys in the 4 x 100-metre relay. He knew I had a background in athletics. They were Malvina High students and the school was happy for my input. At a school level, the four of them were fast. None of them would get very far at the next level, in the 100 metres. So, I worked on their relay baton changes. If you get these

> For God will bring every deed into judgement, including every hidden thing, whether it is good or evil

changes right you can make up a lot of time. I had to explain to them what all the relay lines meant. We measured up their changing area, worked out where each of them should stand, and when to take off.

At zone, you compete against local schools. No one really rated them to get anywhere. We stuck to our plan with our changes and they won, breaking the record. Next came the regional competition among Sydney-wide state schools. Most afternoons we went to the Olympic Stadium warm-up track to train.

The day came for the regional competition. This was a step up. On the day, everyone had spikes, coaches, starting blocks and brand-name track suits. They ran in the heats and came first. We had an hour's break till the final. We debriefed about each of the changes. We all felt they were smooth and we thought we had a chance for a medal. The gun went off. The boys kept their form and won by a few metres. Straight after the race, they talked about one thing, and one thing only. It was almost like they were not bothered by the regional win, but wanted to talk about their chances at State.

We could not do a lot of training that week, except for some run-throughs and baton changes, due to wet weather. It became evident that the fastest individual students did not always win a relay. This is because it all came down to their baton changeovers. We turned up on the day of the heats and there were people everywhere; officials, parents, athletes, even ex-Olympians. I had been to State competitions before, but had never seen anything like this.

They were marshalled to go to the heats. I told the boys to play it safe, with nice smooth changes, and to not run out of their lanes. They ran a good heat and won it. We decided to sit round and watch the other heats progress. We took down heat times and results and who we needed to watch out for in the final. The final was due to be the next day and the relays were the last event of the day. I told them not to get there until midday.

On the day, we headed off to the warm-up track and did some run-throughs. Hours later, the 16 boys' final was marshalled and the boys walked to their different changes. As one of the boys was going to his area, he ran across to me, sitting in the stands. He yelled out to me, nervously, "Which hand do I give it in?" I told him you take it in your right hand and give it in your left.

The starter said, "On your marks, set" and bang! Our first runner ran well. We had never had any bad relay changes in all of the races until our first change in this race. It was terrible and we lost metres. One of the fathers yelled out, "We have no chance!" One of the things I have learnt is you can slowly bring them back. I still remember the second runner made up for lost time and we ran a strong bend; our final runner lifted and overtook another two schools before bringing it home and winning on the finish line. They won gold!

Although the final did not look pretty, they still kept the baton moving. In addition, a lovely gesture was given to me that day. At State, a fifth medal is given, usually for the reserve runner. We had no reserve runner, so they gave me the medal.

Your ability to grow in maturity and move forward is all about passing the baton to future generations, and that's what Paul sought to do with Timothy. This is part of the reason why remembering your creator is profoundly important. Because this is where we see the message alive, in youth. As youth grow old they pass it on to another generation. As Paul says to this young leader: "the things you have heard me say in the presence of many witnesses entrust to reliable people who will also be qualified to teach others" (2 Tim 2:2).

The key is that the baton must be passed to the right people, who in turn will pass it to the right people. In some ways, the baton never stops, it is always being passed on to a new generation of young men and women.

PASSING IT ON

When Paul writes to Timothy, he advises him to reflect deeply on those people who have shaped his Christian upbringing. He reminds Timothy of the significant impact others have made on his Christian walk. From a young age, Timothy had the Christian faith modelled to him. Now he has moved from having a borrowed faith, to owning his faith for himself. Paul is convinced that Timothy has a personal relationship with Jesus; that he recognises the truth about Jesus and is thoroughly equipped to handle the Scriptures. Paul encourages Timothy that, despite what is happening around him in life, he must continue doing the work of God.

I thank God for the godly Christian people He put in my life in my youth. I thank Him for the godly youth leaders who shaped my life in those younger years; for their good habits of accountability, of reading God's word, of praying faithfully, and for being active members of a faithful church. Their example of living out their faith helped me to deal with hardship, rejection, disappointment, health issues and depression in my adult life.

WALK THE TALK

For those of you who are young adults and youth leaders at your own church, I hope and pray that my testimony might encourage you to live out what you teach, or as the saying goes, to "walk the talk", not only for your own sake, but for the sake of those you are ministering to.

A youth leader once approached me, concerned about the drinking culture among some of the youth leaders at their church. I was told that, one night, some of the leaders got drunk and when others questioned them about their behaviour, they replied that the youth group kids were not there, so what the leaders did was irrelevant. The Youth Minister realised that these leaders were lacking in the character and qualities Scripture requires of Christian leaders.

As Paul says to his young leader, Timothy: leaders must be "above reproach" (1Tim 3:2). Later in the book, in chapter 4:16, Paul exhorts Timothy to "watch your life and doctrine closely". It is not enough to simply say you are a Christian; your words and actions must go hand in hand.

As the Teacher in Ecclesiastes warns: "For God will bring every deed into judgement, including every hidden thing, whether it is good or evil" (Eccl 12:14). One of the themes of Ecclesiastes is our accountability to, and our transparency before, God.

Now, while you are young, *this* is the time to form good habits of discipline in your Christian life. To remember God in your youth, is to live for Him your whole life.

FORMING GOOD HABITS

Dimity's birthday is in May and her parents weren't sure whether to send her to school early or to hold her back another year. They decided to hold her back, even though she desperately wanted to go to school. To keep her busy, her parents bought her a violin and offered her violin lessons and she commenced learning the violin at the age of 4. As a teenager, her violin playing progressed. Dimity studied the Suzuki Method which focuses on learning to play by ear, followed by the traditional method of reading music. She toured Europe with orchestras. As a 19-year-old she started her studies at the Conservatorium of Music where she became a professional violinist and played with the Australian Youth Orchestra. Now Dimity works as a music teacher and still plays professionally. The early years in Dimity's violin career laid the foundation for years to come. Those years certainly shaped her as a musician.

Your life is moulded and shaped in your young years.

Remember the statistic I quoted in the introduction: 70% of all Christians come to faith in their teenage years. Your teen years are when you are most likely to establish good patterns and disciplines in your life, when you are not set in your ways like older people.

Towards the end of Ecclesiastes, the Teacher starts to wind up for his conclusion. For youth, he talks about those things we love: light and sweetness. Then, in later years, he talks about those things we hate: the days of darkness, where we have no choices and others make decisions for us (Eccl 11:7-10). He concludes, "So then, banish anxiety from your heart and cast off the troubles of your body, for youth and vigour are meaningless" (Eccl 11:9-10).

The Teacher is saying that the years of your youth should be a time when you don't get anxious. You still have your whole life ahead of you. Anxiety and troubles happen when you're older and you have life experience to help you work through them – not when you're young.

Remember Ecclesiastes follows the journey of a teacher searching for meaning. You may know someone like this, or it could be you. He looks and searches, everything and everywhere. In many ways he is like the lost son of The Old Testament. What a stirring piece of teaching that has as much relevance to the people for whom he initially wrote back then as it does for us today. Invest these fleeting and formative years into your future with Christ.

REMEMBER YOUR TRAINING

Several years ago, I went on holidays to Surfers Paradise with my family and another family. We both had young children. It was a great holiday for the two families. We did a lot, saw a lot, ate a lot, and had a lot of fun. Just as we were leaving to drive to the airport, I put my hand in my pocket to get out the car keys and pulled out the apartment keys, which I'd forgotten to leave at the front desk.

I said to my friends, "Let's not say our goodbyes now, let me drop the keys in first". I ran inside and went to the reception desk to hand in my keys, when I heard someone scream, "Help, help, help!" Without thinking, I ran down the corridor and there was a lady lying on the ground, motionless. The man with her, who I assumed was the husband, started shaking me, crying, "Help me, help me, help me!"

I asked the man whether she had any illnesses. He said she was on heart medication. Time slowed down; it felt like I had stood there for minutes, but it was only seconds. I knelt down to check her pulse, but couldn't find one. I looked at the lady and thought, I've been trained in CPR, I can remember what to do.

I knelt over the lady and did 30 heart compressions, and then two breaths, repeatedly. My friend came in looking for me. I told him to call an ambulance. Fifteen minutes later, the ambos arrived. Two paramedics came in and calmly said to me, "Keep going" while they got their equipment and set it up. Then they took over; half an hour later as they were taking her to the hospital they said to me that when they checked for her pulse, they found a faint one. One of the paramedics said to me, "Because you remembered what to do, you saved her life."

At my First Aid course, I remember thinking I would never, ever have to actually perform CPR on anyone. And in the moment, I was faced with an emergency, I thought I had forgotten what to do. But thankfully, I remembered.

Coming closer to his conclusion, the Teacher in Ecclesiastes urges us to remember. And what he wants us to remember is even more important than how to perform CPR. The Teacher tells us to remember our creator in our youth. Remembering CPR can save someone's short life for a little while, but remembering our creator and living for Him will save our lives for eternity.

Ern and Ruth growing old in their nineties

CHAPTER 10

The consequences of forgetting your creator

"For God will bring every deed into judgement, including every hidden thing, whether it is good or evil."
(Ecclesiastes 12:14)

"Their work will be shown for what it is, because the Day will bring it to light. It will be revealed with fire, and the fire will test the quality of each person's work."
(1 Corinthians 3:13)

The Teacher starts the final chapter of Ecclesiastes by saying "Remember". This isn't like remembering a shopping list. The Teacher calls us, with a sense of urgency, to "Remember your creator in the days of your youth" (Eccl 12:1).

Why is it in your youth that you need to remember? Why not when you're sitting in your nursing home in your nineties? Because the days of your youth make up crucial years of your life. These are the formative years, where your life is shaped. We are called to remember because we so easily forget.

LIFE IS A MIST

Our years of youth are short; as fleeting as a breath, a mist that evaporates in the morning. Remember your creator before the days of trouble, before all these distractions enter your world as you get older, when the distractions get bigger. Your heart may get harder, you may get stuck in your ways. When you are young it is easy to forget about God.

Can people really forget about God? The answer is, yes. The nation of Israel crossed the Red Sea with God's help. They saw God's mighty hand, yet weeks later, while Moses was up Mt Sinai to receive the law from God, the Israelites decided to worship a golden calf. How quickly they forgot about the faithfulness of God. How easily they turned from Him and put their trust in a statue they made with their own hands. The consequences of forgetting our creator God are dire. If we fail to remember our creator in our youth, we will build our lives on a flimsy foundation that will eventually collapse under the weight of life's troubles. Worse still, we will live our lives serving false gods and pursuing meaningless things, as if we do not have to face God's judgement one day.

Young people, the choices you make now impact your future years. What are the things that could distract you from making the right choices? When we reflect on what the Teacher says, we find that each of the seasons of life is different. It's good that someone else has gone through these experiences in life before us. They have reflected on them, and grown from them. We can glean wisdom from the experiences of others to help us navigate the season we are in. What are some of the things that youth need to be reminded of? When are we to remember our creator? Here are some suggestions:

Remember Your Creator

- *When you're thinking or dreaming* **RYC**

- *When you're watching TV* **RYC**

- *When you study* **RYC**

- *When work is overwhelming* **RYC**

- *When you're talking to your friends* **RYC**

- *When you have free time* **RYC**

- *When you play sport* **RYC**

- *When you spend time with your family* **RYC**

- *When you earn and spend money* **RYC**

- *When you're considering your goals* **RYC**

- *When you're driving/travelling* **RYC**
- *When you're planning your future* **RYC**
- *When you're stressed or anxious* **RYC**
- *When you're lonely* **RYC**
- *When you're grieving* **RYC**
- *When you're in financial stress* **RYC**
- *When you're on your own* **RYC**
- *When you're at a party* **RYC**

Remembering your creator will help you think through:

- *What you say on social media.* **RYC**
- *Who should I date?* **RYC**
- *Who should I marry?* **RYC**
- *Should I skip church for a while?* **RYC**
- *How far can I go with my boyfriend and girlfriend physically?* **RYC**

Whatever these things may be or whatever season you are in, "Remember your creator in the **DAYS OF YOUR** *Youth*" (Eccl 12:1).

MAKING WISE CHOICES

The choices you make in your teen years largely determine who you will be when you're older. For instance, choosing to try some activities like drugs, alcohol, porn and social media, can quickly become vices. Their addictive nature means they are destructive habits to form. They can take control of your life and hijack any plans you had for your future.

In 1990, in my first job as a youth minister, I ran a six-week "Christianity Explained" course with two sixteen-year-old boys, Ben and Josh. Something struck them about Jesus at the Scripture seminar that we did at their state high school. They had many questions and we had good discussions. After the course, I asked them both where they were at in thinking about Jesus. Ben said, "I believe it all and I want to become a Christian – but my girlfriend would drop me if I did." She ended up dropping him 2 weeks later anyway. Then it was the HSC (final school year); study, work, travel … "I will, I will" – but he never did. Josh said yes, all those years ago and he's still going strong. Jesus tells a parable about this very thing.

> [28] "What do you think? There was a man who had two sons. He went to the first and said, 'Son, go and work today in the vineyard.'
>
> [29] "'I will not,' he answered, but later he changed his mind and went.
>
> [30] "Then the father went to the other son and said the same thing. He answered, 'I will, sir,' but he did not go.

³¹ "Which of the two did what his father wanted?" (Matthew 21:28-31).

Did Ben really know what Jesus was offering? Or did he know and not really want it? He sounded as though he wanted to accept Jesus as his Lord and Saviour, but continually made excuses as to why he would delay the decision. His words sounded like Yes, but his actions spoke a clear No.

GROWING OLD

The Teacher in Ecclesiastes describes meaninglessness, pleasure, youthfulness, seasons, your foundation, and eternity. After our years of youth come our years of old age. The Teacher describes in detail what it is like to grow old. He calls them the *days of trouble*: "Grinders cease because they are few" - you lose your teeth. "Windows grow dim" - your eyes fail, you will need glasses. "Strong men stoop" - those super sporting heroes will be old and bent over.

Several years ago, I competed in the world Masters' Games. I was 48 and wanted to relive my prime athletic years. I used to do athletics in my youth – I was a high jumper. Just to compete, I needed a cortisone injection, a local anaesthetic injection, physio taping to my ankles, and countless amounts of anti-inflammatory tablets. I suffered for weeks later. The mind was willing, but the body was weakened by age.

I got there early on the day I was competing. I noticed that Clay, one of the seniors when I was a junior, was competing in Long Jump in the 55-60 age-bracket. I thought I'd support Clay by watching him jump. The first guy was a no-show. The next athlete ran down the run-up and snapped a hamstring; he was carried away by paramedics from St John's ambulance. The third guy injured his quad and landed near the shotput area, and the fourth guy landed in the pit, but his back seized up and he was stuck in the sandpit writhing in pain. They were dropping like flies. One man landed short of the pit. The only part of his body that landed in the sand was his face, so they measured from his face-plant. I remember saying to Clay that if he got one jump in he'd win the gold – and he did.

The games were called 'Forever Young' and an athlete died at the games. These games are great, but they show us that old athletes do not have the strength and capability of young athletes. What we once did we cannot, or should not do!

Our present-day sporting greats will one day be physical wrecks. As I was writing this book, I heard that one of the world's greatest sportspeople had passed away. Soccer superstar Diego Maradona passed away age 60. The Teacher in Ecclesiastes says that when you're young, you go out at night, but when you're old you see "dangers in the streets" (Eccl 12:5). You no longer go out at night, you eat dinner at 5 and are in bed by 6!

A season of youthfulness passes and the season of growing old catches all of us. "Almond trees go white" - your hair grows grey. "The Grasshopper drags himself along" - your libido diminishes.

Even those essential things in life that seem to last, like a water jug, (Eccl 12:6) will fade and break. It's like when your new car starts to break down. You think, *but it's new* – then you realise it was once new, but not anymore. Time slips away so quickly. Let our creator God shape your life now.

None of us know when death will find us, but we do not need to seek death out. It finds us all, in the end.[17] We will all die, "we all go to our eternal home" (Eccl 12:5). We will either be going to heaven or hell. The Teacher does not hide this truth from us. For the last time, the Teacher says "meaningless"—life is short: Hevel, breath, a chasing after the wind.

We live in a world without hope. People crave meaning because life is over so quickly, and in the end we all turn to dust. How do we make sense of this short life?

THE STING IS GONE

Before I became a Christian, I had a conversation with a Christian friend and asked what I needed to give up to become a Christian. My friend said, "You misunderstand, George. The Christian life is a hard life but it's a better life. It's what you're gaining." Jesus gives our lives meaning, purpose, forgiveness and grace.

Jesus can do this because there is meaning, purpose and forgiveness, grace. Jesus gives hope even in death.

Death has not reached us yet. One day it will. It matters how we live under the sun, not the sun that keeps us warm, but the Son of God, who saves. And because Jesus rose from the dead, we have the hope of the resurrection. "Death is defeated", the apostle Paul says. It has lost its sting, its power over us (1 Corinthians 15:55).

It was a warm summer's day. A father and his son were driving in their car with the windows down. Out of nowhere, a bee flew in the window and buzzed around inside the car. The young boy started screaming because he had an anaphylactic reaction to bee stings. As the bee flew around the dashboard, the father caught the bee in his hand. A few seconds later, he opened his hand and let the bee go. The bee kept flying inside the car and the boy continued to scream. The bee eventually flew out the window. The boy asked his father why he let the bee go. The father opened his hand and showed his son the sting. He said, "Because I have the sting in my hand, the power of the bee sting is useless." There is one far greater who took the sting out of death for us: King Jesus.

Even the author of Ecclesiastes could not have imagined this good news. Young people, tell your friends about the great hope we have. There is another time in the Bible when we are encouraged: "Remember Jesus Christ raised from the dead" (2 Timothy 2:8). What a great summary of the gospel. Jesus is alive! He has dealt with the issue of death once and for all. What we must do, is remember Him.

The Teacher nails his conclusion. He says we should enjoy what God gives us and be thankful. We should accept that bad things happen in life, and trust God through all seasons of our life. We need to fear God and keep His commandments.

I've always had this emptiness in my life

I tried to fill it with everything and anything

Only Jesus could fill this void

1966 Ford Mustang - Henry Ford

CHAPTER 11

Jesus our rescuer from Judgement

"Fear God and rejoice in his commandments."
(Ecclesiastes 12:9-14)

"Jesus came into the world to save sinners—of whom I am the worst." **(1 Timothy 1:15)**

"You who are young, be happy while you are young, and let your heart give you joy in the days of your youth. Follow the ways of your heart and whatever your eyes see, but know that for all these things God will bring you into judgement."
(Ecclesiastes 11:9)

In Ecclesiastes 12:13, the Teacher concludes: fear God and rejoice in His commandments, for this is the whole duty of humanity. Notice it is not just keeping or obeying his commandments which is sometimes how it is read. Those who follow Jesus will delight in his commandments and how the Holy Spirit enables us to rejoice in them. In 2 Cor 5:17 it says, "Therefore, if anyone is in Christ, the new creation has come: The old has gone, the new is here! "Our creator God made us to be in relationship with him, and we don't find peace in our lives until we are at peace with Him.

MEANING IS FOUND IN JESUS

One young man, Jason, said to me, "There's been this hole that I've had in my life that I could not fill with money, social media, material possessions, sport, or relationships. Nothing filled it until I found Jesus, who saves." Jesus fills the hole in our lives that nothing else fills.

We wonder why some things just don't fit. We are made for eternity, to know our creator, to know the Lord Jesus. Put God first and then everything else can find its proper place.[18] We don't need to look anywhere else for wisdom in life. The cross is where we gain our purpose and find our identity.

On a lonely country road in America, a man's Ford had broken down. His bonnet was up and he stood beside it, scratching his head, not knowing what to do. A motorist stopped and saw he was in distress. He asked if he could have a look under the bonnet. After a few minutes, the man emerged and started the car. They introduced themselves to each other. The man who stopped to help was Henry Ford. The inventor of the car knew how it ought to run: he made it. God has made us, and He knows we function best when we are in relationship with Him. Life will always seem unsatisfying until we know Jesus, who gives us meaning, purpose and hope.[19]

GOD WILL BE OUR JUDGE

Some young people think there aren't any consequences to how we live. But the Teacher tells us it matters how we live, because our every deed will be judged. We will be judged on how well we remember our creator and for our attitude towards Jesus. If you get to the end of your life and have failed to remember, the consequences are eternal (Eccl 12:14).

To remember means more than to just admit that Jesus exits; it means to follow Him and acknowledge that He alone saves. The decisions you make now are what you will give account for when the Judgement Day comes (11:9). Moreover, "no one knows when their hour will be" (9:12) – neither when they will die, nor when Jesus will return. Are you prepared for Jesus to return?

"But about that day or hour no one knows, not even the angels in heaven, nor the Son, but only the Father" (Mark 13:32).

Judgement Day will come for unbelievers. Why did they not trust in Jesus? Believers will also have to give an account of how they have lived their lives for Jesus (1 Corinthians 3:13). The apostle Paul says we are to build our lives on the firm foundation of Jesus, using gold, silver and costly stones that will survive the refining fire of judgement. Let your life be shaped by Jesus.

In life, sometimes you need to ask the question, *what is the wise thing to do?* In the United States in 1829, George Wilson robbed a steam train carrying money. He was captured, tried and found guilty. His sentence was execution by hanging. However, Mr Wilson had many influential friends who were Governors, and they pleaded and petitioned the President of the United States to give Wilson a presidential pardon.

Because of the constant pressure he received, President Jackson gave Wilson a full and unconditional pardon. The death sentence was dropped. You'd think the story ends there…but when officials visited Wilson in prison with the official documents declaring his pardon, George Wilson rejected the pardon!

The law states that if a pardon is rejected, then the death penalty still stands. The pardon is only an offer, it needs to be accepted to come into effect. So even though George Wilson could have walked free, he chose to bear the consequences for his crimes. He died by hanging.

I once told that story to a group of senior students, and a boy yelled out from the back of the class, "That guy's a fool". It is an interesting thought: who would reject a full pardon? There is a pardon offered to each of us, it is written in Christ's blood. Christianity is the only religion that can offer a pardon so we can become right with God.

Here is a story from the Bible, of someone who escaped Judgement and received a pardon. In Luke 23, an incident is recorded about Jesus' death and crucifixion. It was a horrible way to die. It was tortuously slow, it was excruciatingly painful, and in the end you died of suffocation. You could still speak, but it was very painful.

Two thieves were crucified with Jesus that day, one on either side of Him. One of them mocked Jesus, saying, *If you are the saviour, get us out of this predicament!* But the other thief said, *We're thieves: we deserve this. We knew what the consequences would be, but Jesus has done nothing wrong. We are guilty men but this man Jesus is innocent.* The second criminal asked Jesus, "Will you remember me when you are king of your kingdom?"

Jesus replied with these most remarkable words: "I tell you the truth, today you will be with me in heaven."

Notice Jesus didn't say, you *may* be in heaven, I'm not sure. He didn't ask the man what good deeds he had done. He didn't dismiss the man and say, too late mate you will die soon. Jesus said *today* you be with me in heaven. Jesus gave the man this assurance because the man recognised Jesus as King. And because of that, Jesus promised the man would enter into His kingdom. Notice the certainty Jesus gives to this man; it is no *maybe*, but you *will* be with me.

"There was a written notice above him, which read: this is the king of the jews.

One of the criminals who hung there hurled insults at him: "Aren't you the Messiah? Save yourself and us!'

> [40] But the other criminal rebuked him. "Don't you fear God," he said, "since you are under the same sentence? [41] We are punished justly, for we are getting what our deeds deserve. But this man has done nothing wrong."
>
> [42] Then he said, "Jesus, remember me when you come into your kingdom."
>
> [43] Jesus answered him, "Truly I tell you, today you will be with me in paradise." (Luke 23:38-33)

TAKING OUR PUNISHMENT

The theme of remembering appears again. I remember all too well, standing in the science corridor one day, ready to go to class. My mate, Sepan, came up with a great idea: setting off the fire extinguisher! He looked at the two extinguishers and wondered which one to use, the water or the foam. He settled on the foam.

I said to him, "You know you'll get in trouble." He said, "Are you going to stay and watch?" Two other mates, Robert and Ivo, were egging him on as well. "Of course," I replied.

He pulled the pin, pressed the trigger and out came the foam, aimed at two girls, who screamed. It was spectacular to watch. My mates fled the scene like Olympic sprinters running in different directions. While I was lying on the corridor floor laughing my head off, the head of science came out and saw the fire extinguisher next to me. He said, "Statheos, you are busted."

I was sent to the deputy's office, where they asked me if I'd done it. For some dumb reason I said I had, and so I got the cane. I joined my mates at recess and they asked me how many canes did I get: 6 of the best, I said. Sepan was not far from me and I was waiting for one thing, thankyou from him. I was so angry at him. I took his place and hated doing it. I was a lousy substitute. In the passage you just read, Jesus was a willing substitute. The thief went from guilty to innocent, and the good news is that so can we.

The Teacher in Ecclesiastes never had a clear picture, he had only a glimmer of what was to come. He would have longed for the saviour, who would make sense of meaninglessness. Even with all his searching and questioning, the Teacher in Ecclesiastes would never fathom that Jesus was the answer to his question on the meaning of life.

We can know the one who gives us the full picture, the one who brings meaning!

The teacher says, "As no one has power over the wind to contain it, so no one has power over the time of their death" (Ecclesiastes 8:8).

The Teacher would have been blown away by the teaching of Jesus. The Teacher described life as chasing after the wind. He asks: who can control the wind? He says that no one has power over it, yet in the gospels we are told that Jesus calms the wind and the waves. What appears to be an out of control situation, He brings under control. The disciples ask the question, "Who is this man that has power over nature?"

The Teacher questions, "Who has power over death?" The answer is, Jesus—the one who died on the cross and conquered death, once and for all, when He rose to life again.

"Now to him who is able to do immeasurably more than all we ask or imagine". We are not only saved and forgiven by Jesus' death and resurrection. God also promised to give to His followers His Holy Spirit, to help us on this journey as we live for Him. "And you also were included in Christ when you heard the message of truth, the gospel of your salvation. When you believed, you were marked in him with a seal, the promised Holy Spirit" (Ephesians 1:13-14).

I have heard it said: **"Live as if Jesus died yesterday, rose today and is coming back tomorrow."** Young people, share your faith so that your friends and family may know the love that Jesus has for them.

There is only a sense of meaninglessness while we live our short (*hevel*) lives *under the sun*. In heaven, we will know our purpose: to live forever, giving praise to our eternal King.

"*Remember your creator in the*

STUDIES ON ECCLESIASTES

INTRODUCTION

1. Why do so many people wonder why this book is in the Bible?

2. Why do you think the title of this book is *Days of your Youth*?

3. How is this book similar to Adele's song?

4. Who do you think is the author of Ecclesiastes?

5. What does Abel's name mean?

STUDY 1

1. Is there truth behind Eccl 1:2-4?

   "Meaningless! Meaningless!" says the Teacher.

   "Utterly meaningless!

   Everything is meaningless."

   What do people gain from all their labors at which they toil under the sun?

   Generations come and generations go."

2. What do the words *ekklesia* and *qohelet* mean?

3. Why is the word 'meaningless' such a key word in the book?

4. What is the significance of the Cain and Abel story in Genesis 4:8?

5. I have seen all the things that are done under the sun; all of them are meaningless. What is a chasing after the wind?

STUDY 2

1. Eccl 2:1 I said to myself, "Come now, I will test you with pleasure to find out what is good." But that also proved to be meaningless".

   How does the Teacher describe the pursuit of pleasure?

2. What are some of the ways he seeks to define happiness?

3. What is the meaning of the Teacher's statement that "there is nothing new under the Sun"?

STUDY 3

There is a time for everything, and a season for every activity under the heavens:

> *A time to be born and a time to die,*
> *a time to plant and a time to uproot,*
> *³ a time to kill and a time to heal, a time to tear down and a time to build,*
> *⁴ a time to weep and a time to laugh,*
> *a time to mourn and a time to dance,*
> *⁵ a time to scatter stones and a time to gather them,*
> *a time to embrace and a time to refrain from embracing,*
> *⁶ a time to search and a time to give up,*
> *a time to keep and a time to throw away,*
> *⁷ a time to tear and a time to mend,*
> *a time to be silent and a time to speak,*
> *⁸ a time to love and a time to hate,*
> *a time for war and a time for peace. (Eccl 3:1-8)*

1. Why is life described as a season? Look at Genesis 1:14.

2. What do the seasons of life mean?

3. Which season of life are you in now?

4. How can we see the seasons of life as a time of spiritual growth?

5. What are your reflections on a season of war and peace?

6. What does the James passage teach you about suffering? James 1:2-3

7. What is the point behind the mining story?

STUDY 4

1. What do you think of the Teacher's statement that "God has set eternity in the hearts of humans"? Eccl 3:11

2. What does it mean that we want to see the big picture in life, but God is the only one who can provide it?

3. The Apostle Paul says in Acts 17 that Jesus is the only one who can give us eternity. How can he do that?

4. What does it mean for God to give us these things as a gift? (Eccl 2:25-26).

5. "A person can do nothing better than to eat and drink and find satisfaction in their own toil. This too, I see, is from the hand of God, ²⁵ for without him, who can eat or find enjoyment? ²⁶ To the person who pleases him, God gives wisdom, knowledge and happiness, but to the sinner he gives the task of gathering and storing up wealth to hand it over to the one who pleases God. This too is meaningless, a chasing after the wind". How is this passage related to the three pictures that talk about emptiness?

6. What does Eph 2:8-9 teach us?

"For it is by grace you have been saved, through faith—and this is not from yourselves, it is the gift of God— [9] not by works, so that no one can boast. [10] For we are God's handiwork, created in Christ Jesus to do good works, which God prepared in advance for us to do."

STUDY 5

1. How would you describe wisdom? How does Proverbs 1 describe wisdom?

2. In the story of the wise and foolish builders, what makes one wise and the other foolish? (Mtt 7:24-27)

3. What does society tell us to build our life on?

4. Why is your foundation so important in life?

5. What would you say to those who believe Christians do not face storms in life?

6. What does the teacher mean when he says "guard your steps"? (Eccl 5:1)

7. Ecclesiastes 5:15 says we are born naked, we leave this world naked. How true is this?

8. What does Ecclesiastes 5:8-9 teach us about money?

STUDY 6

1. What do we learn from the *60 Minutes* story about Larry winning the Lotto?

2. Why does the rich young man come to Jesus?

3. Jesus tells him to give his money to the poor, if he wants eternal life, why?

4. Timothy Keller says "the human heart is an Idol Factory." What is so profound about this quote?

5. Ecclesiastes 5:10 tells us that "whoever loves money never has enough". Paul says to Timothy that the love of money is the root of all kinds of evil (1 Timothy 6:10). How are these two verses similar?

6. What does 6:12 mean – "we pass like shadows"?

STUDY 7

1. Why do young people need to guard their steps in life?

2. What is the difference between the narrow road and the broad road? (Matt: 7-13-14)

"Enter through the narrow gate. For wide is the gate and broad is the road that leads to destruction, and many enter through it. [14] But small is the gate and narrow the road that leads to life, and only a few find it".

3. The Teacher talks about the 'mouth' and not being led into sin. How can social media be seen as the modern-day mouth?

4. How would you define the word 'hope'?

5. Do you think there is a lack of hope in the hearts and minds of young people? Why or why not?

6. What do you think of Jesus' words "do not worry about tomorrow, for tomorrow will have enough worry on its own"?
   What does the teacher say about wisdom?

7. What does it mean not to pay attention to every word people say?

STUDY 8

1. The Teacher says things can be twisted and cannot be straightened. How is it that Jesus can untwist things like our sin? (Mark 2:1-12)

2. Why does the paralysed man come to Jesus?

3. Why does Jesus forgive the man first?

4. What causes the religious leaders to be upset at Jesus?

5. How is it that we can be forgiven totally?

6. How are we like the paralysed man?

"A few days later, when Jesus again entered Capernaum, the people heard that he had come home. ² They gathered in such large numbers that there was no room left, not even outside the door, and he preached the word to them. ³ Some men came, bringing to him a paralyzed man, carried by four of them. ⁴ Since they could not get him to Jesus because of the crowd, they made an opening in the roof above Jesus by digging through it and then lowered the mat the man was lying on. ⁵ When Jesus saw their faith, he said to the paralyzed man, "Son, your sins are forgiven."

⁶ Now some teachers of the law were sitting there, thinking to themselves, ⁷ "Why does this fellow talk like that? He's blaspheming! Who can forgive sins but God alone?"

⁸ Immediately Jesus knew in his spirit that this was what they were thinking in their hearts, and he said to them, "Why are you thinking these things? ⁹ Which is easier: to say to this paralyzed man, 'Your sins are forgiven,' or to say, 'Get up, take your mat and walk'? ¹⁰ But I want you to know that the Son of Man has authority on earth to forgive sins." So he said to the man, ¹¹ "I tell you, get up, take your mat and go home." ¹² He got up, took his mat and walked out in full view of them all. This amazed everyone and they praised God, saying, "We have never seen anything like this!"

STUDY 9

1. Who are some of the people that have shaped your life and had an impact on your Christian life?

2. Why is it so important to have your life shaped while you are young? What does Paul mean when he says "continue in what you have learnt"? (2 Timothy 3:13-14)

3. The Teacher comes now with this sense of urgency: "remember your creator in the days of your youth". What does this mean?

4. What does (Eccl 9:12) mean, "that no one knows their hour"?

STUDY 10

1. Why do you think youth forget about God in life?

2. How does what we do now affect our future with God? The Teacher reminds us that we will all grow old and face the judge: he gives a list of what growing old will look like. What will it look like?

3. What are some of the truths in these verses? (Eccl 10:17-18).

STUDY 11

1. Why are youth told to remember?

2. What are some of the reasons people give for rejecting Christianity?

3. Look back at the list of vices; which one may you struggle with the most?

4. If the book of Ecclesiastes is about Youth, why does it talk about people growing old?

5. What does the Teacher mean when he says "here is the conclusion of the matter: fear God and keep his commandments"?

6. What are some of the things that people fill their lives with? Why do people seem to want to try everything and anything before they try Jesus?

7. What is so good about the Henry Ford story?

8. What does it mean to live in the way that God intended?

9. Are we ready to face God as the judge?

10. What message does the teacher give for the young? (Eccl 11:9-10.)

"You who are young, be happy while you are young, and let your heart give you joy in the days of your youth. Follow the ways of your heart and whatever your eyes see, but know that for all these things God will bring you into judgement.

[10] So then, banish anxiety from your heart and cast off the troubles of your body, for youth and vigor are meaningless."

STUDY 12

Remember your creator in the days of your youth.

1. What does it mean to remember?

2. How does Ecclesiastes 12:2-7 describe growing old?

"Before the days of trouble come and the years approach when you will say, "I find no pleasure in them"—² before the sun and the light and the moon and the stars grow dark, and the clouds return after the rain; ³ when the keepers of the house tremble, and the strong men stoop, when the grinders cease because they are few, and those looking through the windows grow dim; ⁴ when the doors to the street are closed and the sound of grinding fades; when people rise up at the sound of birds, but all their songs grow faint; ⁵ when people are afraid of heights and of dangers in the streets; when the almond tree blossoms and the grasshopper drags itself along and desire no longer is stirred. Then people go to their eternal home and mourners go about the streets.

⁶ Remember him—before the silver cord is severed, and the golden bowl is broken; before the pitcher is shattered at the spring, and the wheel broken at the well, ⁷ and the dust returns to the ground it came from, and the spirit returns to God who gave it".

What does it mean that we will be judged?
(Eccl12:14)

3. Why does the Teacher conclude with the summation he does? (Eccl 12:13-14).

"Now all has been heard; here is the conclusion of the matter: Fear God and keep his commandments, for this is the duty of all mankind. ¹⁴ For God will bring every deed into judgement, including every hidden thing, whether it is good or evil."

4. Discuss some things you have learnt while studying this book. Remember your creator in the days of your youth!

ENDNOTES

1. Bellamy, Mou and Castle, 2004 Social Influences upon Faith Development. NCLS.
2. I. Provan, *Ecclesiastes, Song of Songs (The NIV Application Commentary)* (Zondervan, 2001), p. 28.
3. Provan p. 28.
4. Provan p. 51.
5. Provan p. 51.
6. Provan p. 51.
7. Plato *Gorgias* 493
8. Leigh Campbell Broken Down Your Life
9. M. Lucado, *When God whispers your name* (Thomas Nelson, 1994),.
10. T. Longman, *The Book of Ecclesiastes* (Eerdmans, 1997).
11. Provan p. 157.
12. Journal Chuck Swindoll overview of ecc 2013.
13. T. Keller, *Counterfeit Gods* (Penguin, 2011), p. 14.
14. D. Kidner, *The Message of Ecclesiastes* (Intervarsity, 1984), p. 23.
15. Provan p. 70.
16. May 30 1792, William Carey spoke at the Baptist Missionary Society.
17. Provan p. 222.
18. T. Longman, *The Book of Ecclesiastes* (Eerdmans, 1997).
19. *God Made You Daily Devotion* Billy Graham 2019.
20. Mars Hill Notes
21. Kirk Patston, SMBC Notes

www.ingramcontent.com/pod-product-compliance
Lightning Source LLC
Chambersburg PA
CBHW071313110426
42743CB00042B/1634

"Everyone setting out on a journey needs a reliable map and this includes young people starting out on life's journey. Ecclesiastes is just such a map. It tells it "like it is," crushing illusion with a heavy dose of reality, and it will save every younger reader who takes it seriously much unnecessary grief and trouble in life. So I warmly commend George Statheos' introduction to this important part of Christian Scripture, confident that its readability and excellent use of example will help bring Ecclesiastes to life for a new generation."

Iain Proven
Professor of Biblical Studies at Regent College Vancouver

We're way more advanced than our parents ever were. We have smartphones that play music, take videos, and tell us which bus to catch. We're more connected than ever before. But the big questions of life still haunt us – How can I be happy? Why am I even here? What's the point of it all? Now, more than ever before, we need to dig into the wisdom of *Ecclesiastes* to answer these questions. But where to begin? I highly recommend *Days of Your Youth* by George Statheos. It is full of wisdom and many funny stories from George's own life. Hopefully we won't make all the silly mistakes he made when he was young.

Sam Chan
Public speaker for City Bible Forum, Australia
Author of *Evangelism in a Skeptical World* and *How to Talk About Jesus (Without Being That Guy)*

Ecclesiastes is for our time and George has so helpfully opened up this precious word to a new generation and addressed their timeless questions. This is a great read and such a helpful resources to teenagers and young adults in particular. I am also glad that the George Statheos I have known for thirty years with his infectious passion to see youth know and grow in Christ is so evident in this book. I highly recommend it.

Ray Galea
Lead Pastor, Fellowship Dubai

Read what 3 teenagers say about *Days of Your Youth*

I was so nervous starting to read Ecclesiastes because as someone who struggles with feeling like life is meaningless and mental health, I thought this book of the Bible would possibly reaffirm that and I was so anxious and I would just spiral, thinking life isn't worth it, if it's meaningless. But God has thankfully humbled me in just a short chapter, that life HAS meaning with Jesus. He provides us the hope, comfort and assurance we all crave. Life under the sun is fleeting and meaningless. But a life with Jesus is purposeful and full of meaning. Thank you, George. I really needed this book to help me open my heart to this.

Steph

As a teenager, finding solid Christian books aimed at my age is very difficult, so this gem-of-a-book was extremely refreshing! *Days of Your Youth* reiterates the importance of growing and nourishing a strong faith during your adolescence and into your adult life. I was personally encouraged by the real-life lines George drew between his experiences and the Word of God. The wisdom George has drawn from the book of Ecclesiastes is written in such a strengthening, entertaining and readable way. Every page is absolute gold!

Samara

Days of Your Youth is an encouraging book for both youth exploring their faith and for youth who want to dig a little deeper into their relationship with God. I was struck by the powerful statistic that 70% of all Christians come to faith in their teen years. This rings true as to how important it is to be establishing a firm foundation in God while we are young. This book helps us as youth to be able to focus on the eternal things rather than the things that will fade away. *Days of Your Youth* breaks down the idea and challenges us to be 'remembering our creator' in all the decisions we make whether big or small. This was an awesome reminder as it is easy to get caught up in the things of this world as a teenager. I loved George's hilarious stories and the way he clearly explained Ecclesiastes and how it can apply to my life.

Luke